MW00983404

Create a Poem

Writing Rhymed and Unrhymed Verse

Mountain
Tall, snow-capped
Towering, skiing, hiking

Poetry

Written by Eleanor W. Hoomes, Ph.D.
Illustrated by Karen Birchak

Other Books by Eleanor Hoomes:

Create-a-Story Series
Create-a-Comedy
Create-a-Drama
Create-a-Fantasy
Create-a-Future
Create-a-Monster
Create-a-Sleuth
Create-a-Utopia
Create-an-Autobiography
Create Heroes and Villains
Laughing Matters
Projects for Young Researchers
Teaching Kids to Write
Young Writers at Work

The purchase of this book entitles the buyer to exclusive reproduction rights of the student activity pages for his or her class only. The reproduction of any part of the work for an entire school or school system or for commercial use is prohibited.

ISBN 978-1-56644-083-7

© 2001 Educational Impressions, Inc.
Second Edition © 2010

Printed in the U.S.A.

EDUCATIONAL IMPRESSIONS, INC.
Hawthorne, New Jersey 07507

Table of Contents

© Educational Impressions, Inc.

 © Educational Impressions, Inc.

Introduction

~POETRY~

Pretty words that sound alike
On each and every line,
Poetry painting pictures,
Of air and space and time.

Love in colors of red and gold,
Spirits done in blue,
Telling of life in fantasy land,
Sometime sad, but true.

Rambling on without end,
Throughout pages and more pages,
Telling of the people who loved
In different times and ages.

Sunshine in poem form,
Bringing smiles to pensive faces,
Causing rainy days to vanish
Forever in some places.

The innermost thoughts
Of life and death
Are recorded here forever
With aching love and bated breath.

Flowers which once stood in gardens tall,
By time now defeated,
Stand only in pages of books,
Telling of lifetimes all completed.

Romances too short and loves too sweet
Are many of the tales;
Hellos and goodbyes abound,
But last, the final farewell.

All of life in poem form,
In books for many ages,
Poems that ramble on, like life,
Through many, many pages.

Renee Ayers, Grade 10

WHAT IS POETRY?

What is Poetry? Poetry is easy to recognize, but difficult to define. It is easy to recognize because its form is distinctly different from the other two forms of literature: prose and drama (although drama may be written in verse). It is difficult to define because there is no single, unique characteristic that all poems share. Many poems make use of emotionally charged, concise, compact, musical language. Readers often are asked to make connections, to take leaps of imagination, and to interpret the meanings found in poems.

Poetry may be narrative, dramatic, or lyric. It may take many forms, such as that of a sonnet, a concrete poem, or a haiku. The speaker in a poem is the person, animal, or object whose point of view is reflected in the poem. The tone of the poem is the attitude of the speaker as revealed by the poem, and the mood of a poem is the atmosphere revealed in the poem.

Figures of speech—such as metaphors, similes, and personifications—and musical devices—such as meter, rhyme, and alliteration—are some of the techniques used by poets to create their poems. The theme(s) of a poem is the general idea, the meaning, or the insight into life that the reader gets from the poem. The themes of some poems are subject to interpretation and, therefore, are not always the same for various readers.

As teachers we cannot expect students to write poetry unless we introduce them to poetry in a pleasurable way. It is best to build on what students already know and currently experience in their popular culture. Look at song lyrics; reread nursery rhymes; look at Dr. Seuss, Shel Silverstein, and Robert Service. Examine commercial jingles and songs and chants used in games, such as jump rope.

I have taken a light-hearted approach to writing poetry in *Create a Poem.* If you wish to introduce more serious poetry to your students, just substitute that type of poetry for the examples that I have provided.

It is unlikely that you will want to use the whole of *Create a Poem* with your students. Pick and choose what you can use; put it together in a different order; use it any way you choose, but do remember, HAVE FUN!

Eleanor Wolfe Hoomes

© Educational Impressions, Inc.

Part One:

Beginning Activities

© Educational Impressions, Inc.

BEGINNING ACTIVITIES

Teacher Directions

At the beginning of the school year, students should be encouraged (required?) to keep a poetry notebook in which they jot down ideas, words, rhymes, descriptions, feelings, reactions, and poems that appeal to them in some way. Poetry notebooks can yield good source material later on when topics are needed for writing. Writing notebooks or journals can also serve the same purpose.

From the beginning stress the importance of writing, rewriting, rewriting, and rewriting for a finished product. Many of the poems in the Student Poetry section were written and rewritten over a period of several months. Share some of your first drafts with your students.

Remind students that their poems may be written in traditional poetry form or in free verse. See Part 3: Types of Poetry for information about traditional poetry and free-verse poetry.

There are three references that are absolutely necessary for students to have readily available when they are writing poetry: a dictionary, a thesaurus, and a rhyming dictionary. An introductory activity where students are required to use all three might be a good idea. You might ask students to find all the rhyming words they can for a list of five to ten words, synonyms for the same words, and all definitions and variations in pronunciation for the same list of words.

STUDENT HANDOUT: RHYTHM AND METER
Give this to the students for future reference. (You will definitely need it for Activity No. 12.)

ACTIVITY NO. 1: ACROSTIC POEMS
There are additional acrostic poems written by students in Part 7. Acrostic poems are a good choice for a first poem. Notice that the examples that I have included were written by two or more students. Below are some possible topics that you might use with students:

Town (City, District)   School   State   Names of Classmates   Animals   Birds

ACTIVITY NO. 2: "I AM" POEMS
"I am" poems take many forms. You might like to choose just one of the three options that I have included in the student activity and do the activity orally as a whole-class activity in which you tell your students which facet of themselves to reveal one step at a time. I have found this system to produce some surprisingly good poems.

ACTIVITY NO. 3: "IF I COULD" POEMS
There is an "If I could" poem included in Part 7. "If I could" poems are generally short. It is important for students to develop their ideas. They definitely need a beginning, a middle, and a conclusion. The following is a suggested formula:

Line 1: If I could…

Line 2: I'd…

The rest of the poem describes what you would do and why.

 © Educational Impressions, Inc.

ACTIVITY NO. 4: WISH POEMS

Wish poems can be realistic or fantastic. A wish poem is included in Part 7. Additional topics for wish poems are listed below.

I wish I were a hummingbird

I wish I were a famous dancer (movie star, athlete, author, singer, etc.)

I wish I were __________________________ (a literary character)

If students are having trouble getting started, suggest that the second line might be the following:

And if I were, I'd ____

ACTIVITY NO. 5: "WHAT IS?" POEMS

"What is?" poems can be used for short poetry-writing assignments throughout the year. The What is happiness? question usually works well.

ACTIVITY NO. 6: JINGLES

You might want to ask the children to listen for jingles the night before this cooperative-learning activity. The following is an example of a possible jingle to advertise Wake-Up!

Wake up to Wake Up!
Start your day off right.
Full of natural, wholesome goodness,
It's a breakfast-eater's delight.

Just add milk;
It's ready to eat.
For breakfast, Wake Up! can't be beat!
Wake up to Wake Up!

Options: Ditties and puns

ACTIVITY NO. 7: RESEARCH A POEM

You might choose to do the research or you might ask your students to it. This activity is good for writing-across-the-curriculum assignments.

ACTIVITY NO. 8: TRAVEL POEMS

I used the travel section from a Sunday newspaper to get the basic information that I used in the example poem, "New Orleans." Travel agencies and travel magazines are also good sources of travel information that students can use.

ACTIVITY NO. 9: PLACE NAMES POEMS

I used a map of Georgia for the place names I used in the example poem. Not all of these names are Native American names; some, like Centralhatchee, are made up to sound like Indian names.

ACTIVITY NO. 10: PARODIES

You might like to start with a parody of TV or radio commercials. You might tape a few for use in class.

ACTIVITY NO. 11: CLASS NAMES

Divide students into groups of four. Assign each group to write poems with their names. After the poems are written, they can be combined into a longer poem using the names of all the students in the classroom. Monitor the writing process closely to make sure no student writes hurtful things about another. The following is an example of this type of poetry:

OUR CLASS

I'm James; this is John.
We're the red-haired twins.
Over there are Charles and Martha,
With their contagious grins.
In the corner is bookworm Doris,
Reading to her cousin Morris.
There are best friends Carter and Turner,
With birthdays that fall in September,
Followed by Heather and Amber,
With the same birthday, the tenth of November.
There's curly-haired, soccer-playing Candy
And her dancing playmate, brown-eyed Sandi.
And last, but not least, we will all agree,
Is our long-suffering teacher, Mrs. McGhee.

ADDITIONAL ACTIVITIES

CRAYONS

Use the colors in a set of crayons for poems on colors. Pass the crayons around and have students choose four (or whatever number you wish) and use them to write and illustrate poems.

CHILDREN'S GAMES

Have students describe a favorite children's game in a poem.

TV SHOWS

Have students describe a TV show they enjoyed at a younger age, thinking about the following questions: When did you watch the show? Under what circumstances did you watch? What other activities were connected with the program? Help them arrange the information into poems.

COWBOY POETRY

Students respond well to this type of poetry, probably because it is usually narrative, traditional in form, and often humorous. The serious side of cowboy poetry depicts life as it was in the early days and the way it is today. The humorous side pokes fun at anything and everything; nothing, particularly politics, is off limits! (Adapted from Doc Stovall and Jerry Warren, cowboy poets) An excerpt from "Cowboys Forever" follows. (Used with permission of Doc Stovall and BMI)

> Where do you find a Cowboy? You know he's a vanishing breed,
> Cause it's tough to live in modern times and follow the Cowboy Creed.
> You'll find him on the prairie if there's any prairie left,
> Or you'll find him somewhere on a horse doing what he does best.

© Educational Impressions, Inc.

Rhythm and Meter

Rhythm is the regular pattern of stressed and unstressed syllables in oral and written language. Poets use rhythm for its musical qualities and to emphasize ideas and feelings.

Meter is the particular rhythmic pattern of a stanza; it is determined by the kind and number of metrical units in a line.

Scansion is the analysis of verse into metrical patterns. The reader **scans** each line of a poem, marking each stressed syllable with a (´) and each unstressed syllable with a (˘). The syllables are then marked off by a (/) into feet. A **foot** is a group of two or three syllables with a particular pattern of stress.

EXAMPLES: Ăróund / thĕ wórld   Énvў / mĕ whén   Í ăm / ălóne

There are several **kinds of feet** in poetry:

Iamb (iambic):	˘ ´	Ăróund
Trochee (trochaic):	´ ˘	Wómĕn
Anapest (anapestic):	˘ ˘ ´	Ĭn ă cár
Dactyl (dactylic):	´ ˘ ˘	Shímmĕrĭng
Spondee (spondaic):	´ ´	Níghtfáll
Pyrrhic:	˘ ˘	Interest/ĭnglў
Amphibrach:	˘ ´ ˘	Ă wóndĕr/fŭl pérsŏn
Amphimacer:	´ ˘ ´	Ríght ănd léft
Monosyllabic:	´	Trúth

Lines are also defined by the **number of feet** in a line:

1. Monometer:	one feet	5. Pentameter:	five feet
2. Dimeter:	two feet	5. Hexameter:	six feet
3. Trimeter:	three feet	5. Heptameter:	seven feet
4. Tetrameter:	four feet	5. Octameter:	eight feet

In traditional poetry lines are grouped into **stanzas.** The metrical pattern and the rhyme scheme usually are repeated in each stanza.

© Educational Impressions, Inc.

Acrostic Poems

An **acrostic poem** is a form of poem in which the letters of the title serve as the initial letters of each line of the poem. Two student examples follow:

EXAMPLE:

BASEBALL

Bouncing, bounding, catch that ball.
All right, all right, watch that call.
Steal to second, then to third—
Easy, easy, home like a bird.
Beat them, beat them, knock them dead.
All right, all right, we're ahead.
Leopards! Leopards! Win the game!
Leopards! Leopards! belong in the baseball hall of fame!

David Adamson, Grade 6
Roger Barber, Grade 5

BABY

Bright little tot,
Always
Blissfully
Yawning and eating.

Betty Parmer Grade 8
Roger Harrod, Grade 5

Try writing your own acrostic poems. For your first, try using your name or the name of a friend. For the second, choose a favorite sport, hobby, or other leisure activity.

© Educational Impressions, Inc.

"I Am" Poems

An **"I am" poem** describes you. It can take many forms. Following are three variations:

VARIATION NO. 1
I am…(name)
I like…
I dislike…
I am…(adjectives)
My favorite dream is…
I would like to talk to…
If I had enough money, I would…
If I could change my name, I would…

EXAMPLE OF VARIATION NO. 1:

RUSSELL SILLS

I am Russell Sills.
I like to camp.
I like to eat.
My hero is Elvin Hayes.

I dislike school.
I dislike work.
I am lazy.
I am bored.
I like summer vacation.

My favorite dream
Is to be a hawk,
Soaring high, soaring free,
With the sun on my back.

I would like to talk to JFK for one hour.
I liked his style, his thoughts on life,
And I would like to be like him.

If I had enough money to buy the world,
I would turn it back to the animals
And send the people into space.

If I could change my name,
I would change it to
Daniel Lee McAdoo, Sr.

Russell Sills, Grade 9

© Educational Impressions, Inc.

VARIATION NO. 2

I am a…
Who likes…
Happiness is…
When I grow up…
In my personal life…
I am…(name)

EXAMPLE OF VARIATION NO. 2:

I am a twelve-year-old boy scout
Who likes playing baseball, working at my computer, and hanging out with friends.
Happiness is vacations from school, especially when spent at the beach.
When I grow up, I want to be
    First of all, a baseball player, and
    Second, a computer engineer.
In my personal life I want to be a husband, a father, and a good citizen.
I am Joey King.

VARIATION NO. 3

I am a…
Who likes…
But dislikes…
REPEAT THE FORMAT OF THE FIRST THREE LINES SEVERAL TIMES.
I am…(name)

EXAMPLE OF VARIATION NO. 3:

I am a boy
Who likes to fish,
But hates squash.
I am a person
Who likes to hunt,
But hates to fight.

I am a Georgian
Who likes to eat,
But hates politics.
I am a human
Who likes to ski,
But hates to work.

I am a student
Who likes P.E.,
But hates classwork.
I am a brother
Who likes to swim,
But hates to write.
I am Donney Hannah.

Donney Hannah, Grade 9

Write your ideas for an "I am" poem in the space below. Then write your poem on other paper.

© Educational Impressions, Inc.

"If I Could" Poems

"If I could" poems start with the phrase "If I could," but beyond that point, they may differ. The poems may be written in traditional verse form with regular meter, rhyme schemes, and stanzas, or they may be written in free verse or even in rhyming free verse. Listed below are several possibilities to help get you started:

If I could live one day over
If I could go anywhere
If I could play any sport to perfection
If I could become president (or CEO, head, chairperson, principal, director, etc.)
If I could be someone else for a day
If I could read the minds of other people
If I could start a charity
If I could be my parents for a day
If I could be ___ (any animal) for a day
If I could become a hero
If I could live under water
If I could fly like a bird
If I could have my own TV show
If I could become famous

EXAMPLE OF AN "IF I COULD" POEM

If I could fly high and free like a red-tailed hawk,
I'd find me one of those thermals and just float
High up there above the earth,
Just drifting, drifting, drifting—
In lazy circles going 'round,
Until I catch the movement of a meadow mouse,
Way down there on the ground,
Realize that I skipped lunch,
And dive straight for my supper.

Write your ideas for an "If I could" poem in the space below. Then write your poem on other paper.

____

____

____

____

____

____

____

© Educational Impressions, Inc.

Wish Poems

Wish poems take many forms, but they should all include the phrase "I wish" somewhere in the poem. Wish poems may be written in traditional verse with regular meter, rhyme schemes, and stanzas, or they may be written in free verse or even in rhyming free verse.

EXAMPLES:

THREE WISHES

If wishes three you gave to me,
I'd wish for forgiving tolerance
Among all peoples of the earth.
I'd wish for an environment clean
And natural, and last of all,
I'd wish for all a lasting peace.

I WISH

I wish I could,
I wish I would,
Always do the
Things I should.

Wish poems may be written with a theme: Colors, Flavors, Animals, Textures, etc.

Complete the following poem starters:

I see the stars come out tonight;
I make a wish, my eyes closed tight;
I wish that ______________________

____

I wish I could tell you my secret

____

____

____

I wish you would keep my secret

____

____

____

I wish I were a summer breeze

____

____

____

I wish I would win the lottery

____

____

____

I wish that I were ten years older

____

____

____

I wish that summer vacations lasted 6 months

____

____

____

I wish I were a king

____

____

____

© Educational Impressions, Inc.

"What Is?" Poems

"What is?" poems start with a question: What is happiness? What is anger? What is love? They can take any form and be any length.

EXAMPLE:

WHAT IS HAPPINESS?

Happiness is a warm summer day,
An ice-cream cone along the way.
It's a sprinkler to run through,
A dip in the pool,
A good friend to share them with—
That's really cool!

Use the following suggestions to help you create your own "what is?" poems or use ideas of your own.

What is happiness?
What is green (any color)?
What color is happiness?
What is friendship?
What is a grandmother?
What is bliss?
What is loyalty?
What is honesty?
What is fun?

What is contentment?
What color is grief?
What color is anger?
What is jealousy?
What is a grandfather?
What is love?
What is truth?
What is hunger?
What is pain?

What is anticipation?
What color is envy?
What is disappointment?
What is home?
What is surprise?
What is honor?
What is beauty?
What is school?
What is trust?

Jingles

A **jingle** is a short, catchy song or piece of verse. Musical jingles are used in advertising and in theme songs, especially for children's programs. They are also used in children's games, such as jump rope.

In the space below, write your favorite jingle.

Your group of three or four has been asked to write a jingle for a new breakfast cereal, which has been named Wake Up! Below is a list of rhyming words you might like to use.

fight	light	might	night
sight	daylight	limelight	insight
tight	delight	ignite	bright
knight	right	starlight	fortnight
eyesight	tonight	oversight	fright

In the space below, write your jingle for Wake Up!

 © Educational Impressions, Inc.

Research a Poem

Ideas for writing poems come from many sources. Use newspapers, magazines, reference books, informational programs on TV and radio, websites, and/or your store of knowledge. For each topic you research, list five to ten bits of interesting information in a notebook or on 5" x 8" index cards. This will give you several sources to draw from when you are stuck for ideas.

The information on cardinals came primarily from the following books: *Bird Watching for Dummies, Peterson Field Guide for Eastern Birds,* and *Common Birds of Atlanta* (see below):

CARDINALS:

1. Cardinals are among the earliest songbirds to begin their mating rituals.
2. The male cardinal is red.
3. The male is aggressive when contending for domain.
4. The male cardinal is very nurturing. His nurturing instinct is so strong that he will even feed other creatures' offspring! One photographer documented a male cardinal feeding goldfish in a backyard pool.
5. During courtship the male cardinal brings his sweetheart gifts of seeds and feeds them to her in a "courtship kiss."
6. Cardinals sing, mostly in spring, a pleasant "Kyeer, Kyeer," "What-cheer, What-cheer," "Whoit, Whoit, Whoit," "Purty, Purty, Purty," or "Birdy, Birdy, Birdy."
7. It is against the law to kill, harm, or even own the feather of a songbird.

RITUAL

In springtime, early springtime,
The cardinals return.
Scarlet macho males
Sing warning songs to the competitors:
"Keep away from my territory;
Keep away, Keep away, or therefore,
You'll be the gift the cats leave,
For the humans at their front door."

Followed by love songs to the pretty females,
"Purty! Purty! Purty! Birdy! Birdy! Birdy!
Hey, Sweet Mama. Yes, you, Cool Chick.
Wanna build a nest with these nice sticks?"
Then like a courting lover
Bringing chocolates and roses to his sweetheart,
Mr. Cardinal entices the future Mrs. Cardinal
With gifts of seeds garnered from the humans'
garden cart.

Then they build their nest, absolutely precise,
Raise their fledglings with great sacrifice,
And live happily ever after in Red Bird Paradise.

Roger Tory Peterson. *Peterson Field Guides, Eastern Birds.* Boston: Houghton Mifflin Company, 1980.
Bill Thompson III. *Bird Watching for Dummies.* IDG Books, 1997.
Jim Wilson and Anselm Atkins. *Common Birds of Atlanta.* Hexagon Publications, 1999.

© Educational Impressions, Inc.

Research a Poem

See how simple it is. Try writing a researched poem. Write it in free verse or rhyming verse. Length does not matter. You will notice that I did not use all seven bits of information I listed. It is better to have more information than you need than not to have enough.

Subject I Have Chosen: ________________________________

List five to ten bits of information about the subject you have chosen for your poem.

1. ________________________________
2. ________________________________
3. ________________________________
4. ________________________________
5. ________________________________
6. ________________________________
7. ________________________________
8. ________________________________
9. ________________________________
10. ________________________________

Write your research poem in the space below.

© Educational Impressions, Inc.

Travel Poems

The following is an example of a poem about a popular travel destination.

NEW ORLEANS

Watch Mardi Gras parades on Bourbon Street.
Have a portrait quick-sketched in colored chalks on Jackson Square
While you watch mimes, magicians, and musicians
Perform for pocket change nearby.
Ride the streetcars through the Garden District
To see the antebellum mansions surrounded by wrought-iron fences.
Smell the spicy fixin's for Creole and Cajun specialties
Early in the morning at the French market.
Then buy your T-shirts and trinkets at the nearby flea market.
See marine life eye to eye at the Aquarium of the Americas,
At the mouth of the mighty Mississippi River.
Then take a riverboat on the muddy Mississippi,
Returning to Café du Monde for hot chocolate and sugar-coated beignets.
And, if you're lucky, you might follow a jazz band back to your inn.

Now compose your own travel poem. Use travel sections from the Sunday newspapers, travel magazines, or travel information provided by chambers of commerce or travel agencies to learn about a place of interest to you. It could also be a place that you have visited.

List several places you enjoyed visiting or would like to visit. Then put a check next to your choice.

_______________________ _______________________

_______________________ _______________________

_______________________ _______________________

List at least five facts about the place you have chosen for your poem.

1. _______________________
2. _______________________
3. _______________________
4. _______________________
5. _______________________
6. _______________________
7. _______________________

Write your travel poem on another sheet of paper. Perhaps you would like to illustrate your poem.

© Educational Impressions, Inc.

Place Names Poems

Use a local, country, or world map. Make a list of place names that appeal to you for some reason. These names might be names of cities, towns or villages, countries, districts, rivers, lakes, mountains, deserts, or regions. You might choose names for their sounds, because you would like to visit there, or for any reason at all. You might even close your eyes, put your finger on a place, open your eyes, and write down all the names in the vicinity of your finger.

After you have a list of several place names, study the list. Then start playing with them on paper—arranging them and then rearranging them until you like what you have done. Add other words until you have a poem.

EXAMPLE:

Centralhatchee, Chattachoochee, Muscogee, and Willachoochee.
Dahlonega, Tallaposa, Chicamauge, and Allatoona.
Ocmulgee, Cherokee, Hiawasee, and Oconee.
Tallulah, Kennesaw, Montezuma, and Omaha.
Ocilla, Cohutta, New Echota, and Nahunta.
Georgia legacies, all—

★Atlanta
Georgia

List your choice of place names.

_______________ _______________
_______________ _______________
_______________ _______________
_______________ _______________

Write your poem in the space below.

____
____
____
____
____
____
____
____
____
____
____
____

 © Educational Impressions, Inc.

Parodies

A **parody** is a literary or musical work in which the style of an author or a work is closely imitated in a lighthearted manner. Poems and songs are good choices for parodies. The form, style, meter, and rhyme scheme is followed in a poem. In a song, in addition to the form, style, meter, and rhyme scheme, the tune is also closely followed.

EXAMPLE:

HERE COMES CHEETAH SWISHY TAIL
(Based on *Here Comes Peter Cottontail)*

Here comes Cheetah Swishy Tail,
Stalking down the jungle trail.
Swish-er-ly, swash-er-ly,
Summer's on its way.

Bringing every girl and boy,
Buckets full of summer joy.
Here to make your,
Summer bright and gay.

Mostly by *Victoria Jordan,* Age 4, with the help of her Gran

Make a list of poems and/or songs that you might parody. Think of current popular songs, "golden-oldies," nursery rhymes, favorite poets (such as Shel Silverstein or Robert Service), or even commercial jingles. Then choose one from your list and write your parody.

Class Names Poems

You can use the names of students in your classroom to write poems. You might want to start with the names of four students, as I did in the following example.

EXAMPLE:

FOUR FRIENDS

I'd like you to meet
The four students in Mrs. Connor's class
Who sit close to me.
There's Angelina, the brilliant ballerina;
John, who loves to joke and have fun;
Brandon, who reads books about the Yukon;
And fleet Bridget, the fastest girl on her street.
These four friends make my school day complete.

I used a rhyming dictionary to find some of the rhymes I used in the poem above. A rhyming dictionary can make writing rhyming poetry much easier.

List the names of all your classmates on another sheet of paper. How can you use them in a poem or a series of poems? Use the space below to write your poem or poems.

 © Educational Impressions, Inc.

Part Two:

The Shape of Poetry

Teacher Directions

Probably the most distinctive characteristic of poetry is its shape. Although there are many different ways to shape poetry, it is the fact that poetry is formed on the page differently from prose that immediately tells readers that they are reading poetry. As the readers read the poems, other elements of poetry become apparent.

You might like to display poetry of many different shapes on the bulletin board, the walls, the windows, the doors, suspended on poster boards with fishing line or twine from the classroom ceiling, and in other parts of your school. At first the poetry might be favorite poems of the students, but they should be replaced with works *by* your students as soon as possible.

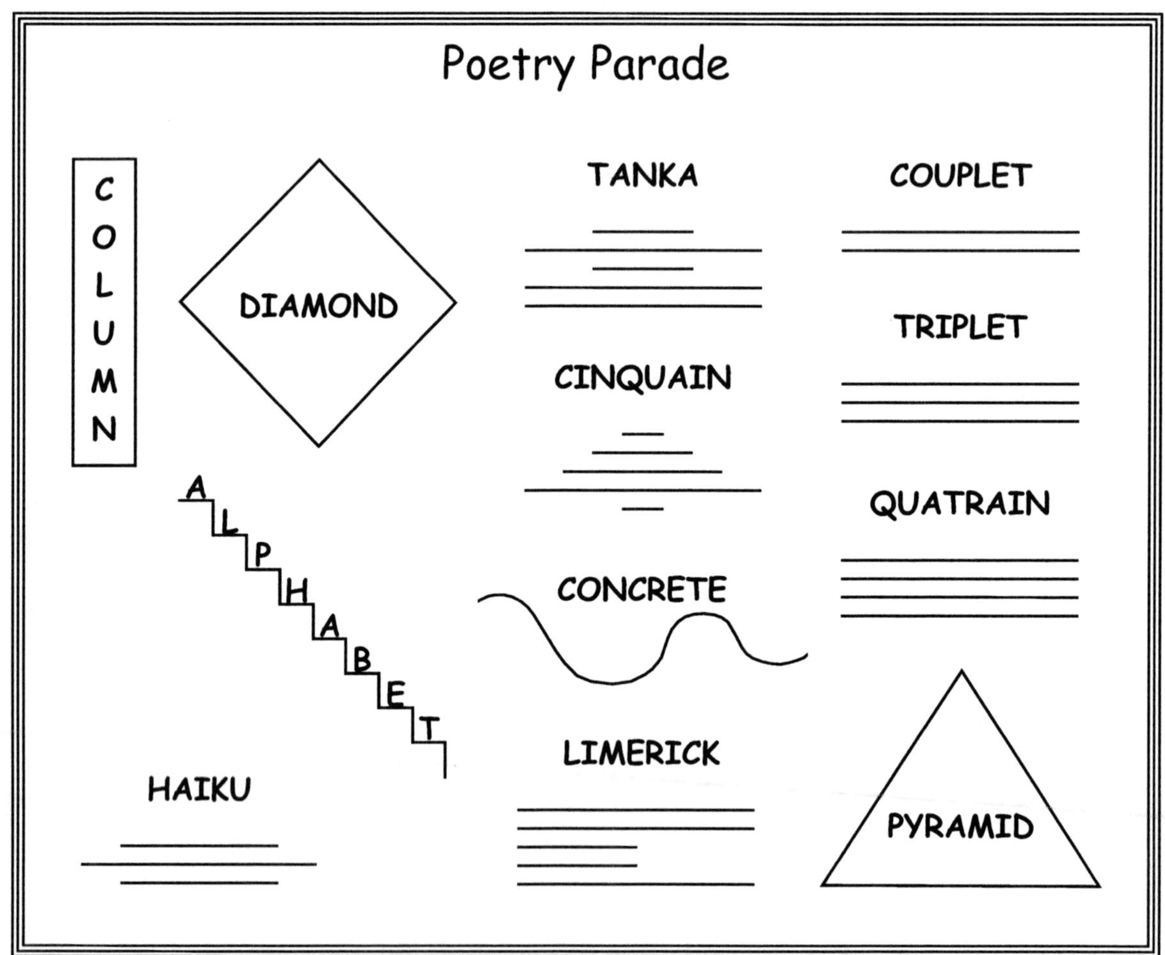

ACTIVITY NO. 12: STANZAS

I have given examples of couplets, tercets (triplets), and quatrains in the student activities. See Part 7 for additional poetry, especially "Them Smart Kids," written in quatrains, and the quatrain "Myself." Continue to encourage students to use a dictionary, rhyming dictionary, and thesaurus.

 © Educational Impressions, Inc.

Show students how choices about the arrangement of lines can change the shape of a poem. Note that I have used the same material in "Summer" for a tercet and a quatrain in Activity 12 and for a tanka in the teacher directions for Activity 14. You might like to use one of the example poems and ask students to change the arrangement of the lines. Then discuss if this changes the meaning of the poem and whether or not it improves it.

The following is an example of a sestet:

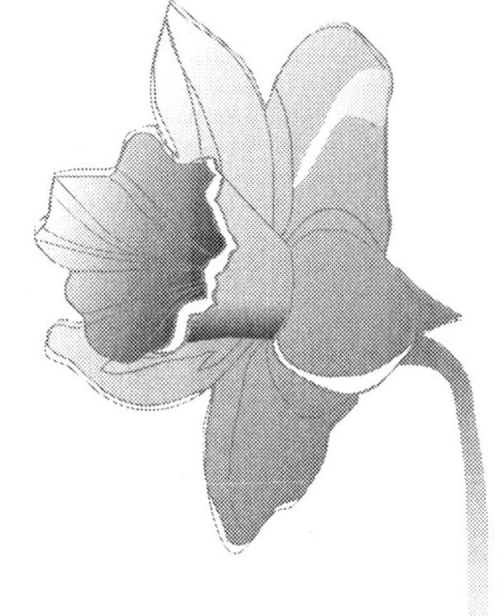

BUDS GO BOOM

In the flower box, I declare,
Buds go boom everywhere!
I wish I could have heard the boom
When all the buds burst into bloom!
When all the buds burst into bloom!
I wish I could have heard the buds go boom-da-de-boom!

Jean Taylor, Grade 6

ACTIVITY NO. 13: HAIKU

Students probably will be familiar with the 3-line requirement of haiku, but may be unaware of the syllable convention of 5-7-5. Because syllables have more significance in Japanese than in English, American writers do not always follow the strict 17-syllable rule. However, when a haiku in English conforms to the 5-7-5 rule, it just sounds right.

Remind students that the magic of haiku lies in the power of suggestion. Haiku portrays a moment of vivid perception. **Word choice is everything** in writing good haiku.

ACTIVITY NO. 14: TANKA

Tankas are harder to create than haikus simply because they are longer. They have 31 syllables instead of 17: 5-7-5-7-7. Tankas can deal with more complete images than haikus. You might have students turn some of their haikus into tankas. An example of a tanka follows:

Roses blooming red,
A winged carmine cardinal,
Crimson tomatoes,
Scarlet scented begonias,
All the red of mid-summer.

ACTIVITY NO. 15: SYNONYMOUS CINQUAINS

The following is a possible pattern.

Line 1: 1 word	Toy,	Toni,
Line 2: 2 words	Fun, games,	Petite, pretty,
Line 3: 3 words	Laughing, playing, romping.	Smiling, sharing, caring,
Line 4: 4 words	Sharing with a friend,	Always a good companion,
Line 5: 1 word	Plaything.	Friend!

Mention to your students that there are other patterns. Another, more difficult, pattern for a synonymous cinquain follows:

Line 1: 2 syllables	Mary,
Line 2: 4 syllables	My one sibling,
Line 3: 6 syllables	Considerate and kind,
Line 4: 8 syllables	A princess from Rome, Tennessee.
Line 5: 2 syllables	Sister!

A thesaurus is a necessity for students when they are writing synonymous cinquains.

ACTIVITY NO. 16: PYRAMID POEMS

Pyramid poems are fun. It is easier to use words to determine line lengths than to use syllables. However, you may have some students who are challenged by the syllable pattern.

Teacher,
Swing me.
Push me higher;
Swing me up higher
So I can touch rainbows,
So I can kiss golden eagles,
So I can reach the shining stars,
Read three books and return to Planet Earth,
A transformed reader who has traveled the Milky Way.

ACTIVITY NO. 17: DIAMOND POEMS

Diamond poems are challenging. They can have 5, 7, 9, or more lines, but they should always be composed of an uneven number of lines. The following example conforms to the pattern for a 7-line diamond poem.

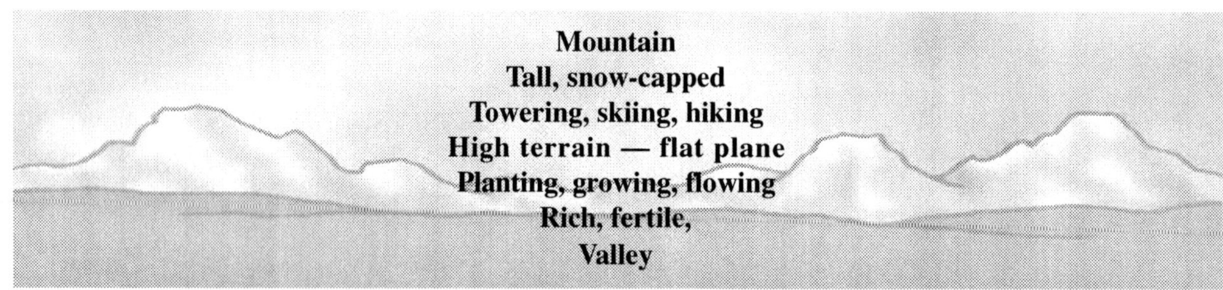

Mountain
Tall, snow-capped
Towering, skiing, hiking
High terrain — flat plane
Planting, growing, flowing
Rich, fertile,
Valley

ACTIVITY NO. 18: COLUMN POEMS

Some students enjoy the challenge of column poems, but others feel that they are too restrictive. I have found them to be useful in focusing students on choosing that one absolutely correct word.

ACTIVITY NO. 19: ALPHABET POEMS

Alphabet poems are simply exercise poems. They make a good dictionary and/or thesaurus activity and are challenging for some students. It is highly unlikely that you will get outstanding poems from them; therefore, it is best to treat them as novelty or "fun" poems.

 © Educational Impressions, Inc.

ACTIVITY NO. 20: CONCRETE POEMS

Students can and do write some good concrete poetry. Concrete poetry communicates visually as well as verbally. The first example, "The Merry-Go-Round," can be read in two ways: You can start with the outer circle with "I love," or at the inner circle with "I like." The second example should be read from the inside to the outside. These poems make a great display.

ACTIVITY NO. 21: LIMERICKS

The limerick is a form of poetry familiar to many students. You might like to teach the activity on limericks early in your poetry unit because limericks do catch the interest of students. Have students write one, two, three, or four lines of limericks for other students to finish. They might also write ending lines for students to begin.

ADDITIONAL ACTIVITIES

POPULAR SAYINGS

Use popular sayings or their beginnings as the first part of poems. Encourage students to think of unusual rhyming endings.

EXAMPLES (Based on "He who hesitates is lost."):

"He who hesitates is lost,"
I've often heard said,
But it's been my experience,
Especially when turning right on red,
That he who doesn't hesitate,
______________________________.

He who hesitates
Before crossing the way
Lives to hesitate
Another day.

POSSIBLE ENDINGS TO THE FIRST EXAMPLE:

May receive a knock on the side of the head.
May be run over by a moped.
May be moaning in the roadbed.
Is rightly called knucklehead.
May spend fifteen days in bed.
May soon see his blood shed.

DEAD POET'S SOCIETY

If you are working with older students, show the movie *Dead Poet's Society*. (NOTE: If you don't have time or if "the powers that be" frown upon showing this movie in class, show only those parts that show the students composing poetry.)

POETRY WORKSHOP

Divide students into small groups. Arrange for them to conduct poetry workshops with younger students. Spend some time training them before the workshops. Remember your teacher-training seminars!

POETRY READINGS

Invite upper-class students to read poetry they have written. Invite teachers, administrators, local officials, newspaper reporters, etc., to come to your classroom to read their favorite poetry.

Stanzas

A **stanza** is a fixed form in poetry that is written in a regular, orderly manner. Poets shape stanzas by repeating the same number of lines and using the same meter pattern. Usually, the same rhyme scheme is used. Stanzas may be compared to paragraphs in prose. Often each stanza deals with one main idea. Stanzas are named according to the number of lines contained in them:

Couplet: 2 lines
Tercet (triplet): 3 lines
Quatrain: 4 lines
Cinquain: 5 lines
Sestet (sextet): 6 lines
Septet (heptastich): 7 lines
Octave (octet): 8 lines

COUPLET

A couplet has two lines. A rhyming couplet is a two-line stanza that rhymes. Longer poems may be written in rhyming couplets. (See the second example.) Rhyming couplets are also used as endings for poems (or other literary genres) because they have a final sound.

EXAMPLE:

When I go home from school each day,
I eat a snack and then I play.

EXAMPLE OF A QUATRAIN IN RHYMING COUPLETS:

I crawl in bed and yell, "Goodnight."
I look outside; the moon is bright.
I make a wish. Will it come true?
I do not know. Perhaps you do.

You might like to use some of the following rhyming words in writing couplets:

freewheel	peel	kneel	heal	real	feel	heel
deal	he'll	peal	reel	spiel	squeal	veal
wheel	oatmeal	ordeal	congeal	schlemiel	piecemeal	zeal
appeal	newsreel	conceal	genteel	reveal	teal	steal
cartwheel	snowmobile	glockenspiel	imbecile	cockatiel	automobile	chenille

TERCET OR TRIPLET

A tercet, or triplet, is a three-line poem or a three-line division in a longer poem. It may or may not rhyme. The following are possible rhyme schemes for tercets:

1.	2.	3.
a	*a*	*a*
a	*b*	*b*
a	*b*	*a*

 © Educational Impressions, Inc.

EXAMPLES:

SUMMER

Roses blooming red I see,	*a*
Cardinals on the wing so free,	*a*
And children playing by the sea.	*a*

MRS. ROBIN RED-BREAST

Mrs. Robin Red-breast	*a*
In a fit of anger said,	*b*
"You sit on the nest!"	*a*

Angelia Hoomes, Grade 8

THE LAST DAY OF SCHOOL

Impatiently waiting at my desk	*a*
Tick-tock, tick-tock, tick-tock,	*b*
Won't you hurry up, Mr. Clock?	*b*

QUATRAIN

A quatrain is a four-line, usually rhyming, poem or a four-line division in a longer poem.

POSSIBLE RHYME SCHEMES

1. a	*2. a*	*3. a*	*4. a*	*5. a*	*6. a*	*7. a*
a	*a*	*b*	*b*	*b*	*b*	*b*
a	*b*	*a*	*b*	*c*	*c*	*c*
a	*b*	*b*	*b*	*c*	*a*	*b*

EXAMPLES:

NATURE

I'm the sun, shining down bright.	*a*
I'm the rain, pouring down with all my might.	*a*
I'm the gentle wind just beginning to blow.	*b*
I'm the moon, sending down a cloudless glow.	*b*

Jane Nutt, Grade 9

SUMMER

Roses blooming red I see,	*a*
Cardinals on the wing so free,	*a*
Children playing by the sea,	*a*
Signs of summer, all three.	*a*

SUMMER

On a sizzling hot summer day,	*a*
Among the dappled shadows,	*b*
On the banks of meandering Crookneck Creek	*c*
My friends and I play hide-and-go-seek.	*c*

Create your own quatrains. Label each line to show the rhyme schemes.

______________________________	____	______________________________	____
______________________________	____	______________________________	____
______________________________	____	______________________________	____
______________________________	____	______________________________	____

Haiku

Haiku is an ancient Japanese verse form. It has a total of three lines and seventeen syllables and usually does not rhyme. Haiku is poetry and, as such, is meant to express and evoke emotion.

HAIKU PATTERN

5 syllables	1 2 3 4 5
7 syllables	1 2 3 4 5 6 7
5 syllables	1 2 3 4 5

Haiku may be serious, humorous, satirical, charming, deep, or light. Because of the brevity of haiku, certain conventions are used:

1. Longer ideas and concepts may be suggested by a word or short phrase.
2. Connections are skipped, but the reader supplies the missing connections.
3. Usually two ideas are associated or compared.
4. *Ki* (season) is used to indicate the time of year. In nearly all haiku, a word or expression is used to indicate the time of year and becomes a background for the image(s) evoked by the haiku. A *kigo* (season word) may be definite (winter cold) or suggested (cherry blossoms).
5. There is more emphasis on emotion than on behavior or action.
6. Natural phenomena are used to reflect human emotions.
7. Words which are not needed to make the sense clear are omitted.

EXAMPLES:

A deer running wild ____
Is as free as the spring wind ____
Unless beef goes up. ____

Donney Hannah, Grade 9

The soaring sea gulls ____
Against a summer blue sky ____
Gliding on the breeze. ____

Russell Sills, Grade 9

Count the syllables in the above lines.

Write your own haiku poems in the space below. Count your syllables.

______________________________ ____ ______________________________ ____
______________________________ ____ ______________________________ ____
______________________________ ____ ______________________________ ____

______________________________ ____ ______________________________ ____
______________________________ ____ ______________________________ ____
______________________________ ____ ______________________________ ____

© Educational Impressions, Inc.

Tanka

Tanka, another Japanese form of poetry, starts like haiku but has two additional lines for a total of 31 syllables: 5-7-5-7-7. This five-line poem does not rhyme.

Think of abstract words, such as love, hate, joy, loyalty, freedom, liberty, trust, happiness, and any aspect of nature. Next think of images that illustrate this abstract idea. Then describe the mental images without being concerned about the number of syllables; you just want to get your ideas down as quickly as possible at this point. After you have your images on paper, rearrange them into the tanka pattern. You may have to add or subtract words or substitute synonyms for longer or shorter words to achieve the correct length of your lines.

EXAMPLE:

Gold sunbeams softly ____
Caress the world around me ____
With soft yellow light. ____
They warm the crippling darkness ____
Inside the lonely places. ____

Count the syllables in the above lines.

POSSIBLE TOPICS FOR TANKA:

moonlight	rivers	home	seasons	oceans
birds or animals	lakes	clouds	mountains	storms

Write your own tanka poems in the space below. Count your syllables. Illustrate your poems.

________________________________ ____
________________________________ ____
________________________________ ____
________________________________ ____
________________________________ ____

________________________________ ____
________________________________ ____
________________________________ ____
________________________________ ____
________________________________ ____

© Educational Impressions, Inc.

Synonymous Cinquains

A **cinquain** is a five-line poem. A **synonymous cinquain** follows a specific pattern.

SYNONYMOUS CINQUAIN

1 word: Subject and title
2 words: Adjectives
3 words: "-ing" Verbs
4 words: Descriptive words (Can be a phrase or a list of describing words)
1 word: Synonym for subject/title

EXAMPLES:

Hypocrite,
Sanctimonious, two-faced,
Cheating, lying, pretending,
Can never trust one,
Phony.

Husbandry,
Careful, judicious,
Protecting, controlling, farming,
Careful management of animals,
Conservation.

Use the following pairs to write your own synonymous cinquains:

Toy-Plaything Rose-Flower Name-Friend Name-Brother (Sister, Mother, Father, Etc.)

____

____

____

____

____

____

____

____

____

____

 © Educational Impressions, Inc.

Pyramid Poems

A **pyramid poem** is shaped like a pyramid. The number of lines can vary in a pyramid poem, from three to as many as you need to complete the sense of the poem. A pyramid poem may rhyme or not. There are two possible patterns for the length of each line.

Line 1: 1 word or syllable
Line 2: 2 words or syllables
Line 3: 3 words or syllables
Line 4: 4 words or syllables
Line 5: 5 words or syllables
Line 6: 6 words or syllables
and so on.

EXAMPLES:

On
Tuesday I
Read a book
About far flung lands
And a fairy princess and
A daring hero, who saved the
Princess. But if I had written the
Book, the princess would have saved the hero.

Spring,
A p p l e s
With green leaves
And buzzing bees.

Now try writing pyramid poems. Stretch your imagination and have fun with them. Use images (word pictures) to convey your main ideas.

____

____

____

____

____

____

____

____

____

____

____

____

© Educational Impressions, Inc.

Diamond Poems

A **diamond poem** is shaped like a diamond. There are many variations in the way that diamond poems can be written. The two common elements are that of shape and the use of antonyms for the first and last lines. They should always be composed of an uneven number of lines: 5, 7, 9, and so on. One common pattern for a diamond poem follows:

Line 1: 1 noun
Line 2: 2 adjectives
Line 3: 3 "-ing" words
Line 4: 4 words showing change
Line 5: 3 "-ing" words
Line 6: 2 adjectives
Line 7: 1 noun (an antonym of the noun in the first line)

EXAMPLE:

Mountain
Tall, snow-capped
Towering, skiing, hiking
High terrain—flat plane
Planting, growing, flowing
Rich, fertile
Valley

Use the following pairs of antonyms (or supply your own) to write a diamond poem:

Baby/Adult	Fire/Ice	Youth/Elder
Day/Night	Summer/Winter	Earth/Sea
Toy/Tool	Spring/Autumn	Valley/Mountains

 © Educational Impressions, Inc.

Column Poems

A **column poem** is composed of one word per line. There is no required rhyme scheme. The lines may rhyme, but it is not necessary.

EXAMPLE:

FOOTBALL

Crash!
Bash!
Gain!
Pain!
Cleats!
Completes!
Scores!
Roars!

David Hosey, Grade 9

There are no required number of lines for a column poem. They may be as short as three or four lines or they may be much longer.

Provide a title to each of the following poem-starters and finish them with at least four more lines each. If you prefer, you may use one or more as poem-enders instead.

____

Children
Playing,
Happily
Waiting.

____
____
____
____

____

Flower
Power!

____
____
____
____

____

Presents,
Abundant!

____
____
____
____

____

Lights,
Delight!

____
____
____
____

© Educational Impressions, Inc.

Alphabet Poems

Alphabet poems may begin with any letter of the alphabet, but they must continue in alphabetical order from that chosen letter.

ALPHABET STEP POEM

In this type of poem each line is only one word and the lines are done in a step pattern.

EXAMPLE:

Babies
Can
Destroy
Everything.
Feckless,
Grabbing
Hands.
Inquisitive,
Joyful,
Kinetic,
Lovable
Monkeyshines.

ALTERNATE TYPE OF ALPHABET POEM

Start with any letter of the alphabet. You may skip letters, but the first letter of each line and all words within each line must be in alphabetical order.

EXAMPLES:

Antique bureaus
Catching dust
Elude fastidious
Housekeepers.

Greedy hands,
Impolite manners,
Offensive perfumes
Rebound.

Create your own alphabet poem using either pattern. See how long you can carry it out and still have it make sense. Challenge yourself to write a poem using all 26 letters of the alphabet! Jot your ideas in the space below. Write your poem on another sheet of paper.

© Educational Impressions, Inc.

Concrete Poetry

A **concrete poem,** also known as a shape poem, is one whose shape suggests its subject. Concrete poems are not only creative, but also fun to do. They do not require meter, rhyme, or a specified number of words or syllables. The only requirement is to describe an image, a feeling, a thought, or a situation in a shape that reinforces that image, feeling, thought, or situation.

EXAMPLES:

I love to ride the merry-go-round right here in the old fairgrounds. I like the way the music sounds, holding me completely spellbound.

I'm running around in circles like a chicken with its head cut off. If something doesn't relieve my stress very soon, I think I'll just blast off!

Create your own concrete poems. Use one of the following suggested topics or one of your own:

Skiing on the beginners slope
Bouncing on a trampoline
Watching a tennis match
A car on a narrow mountain road
A speedboat
A storm
Love or friendship
Jumping rope

Jot your ideas in the space below. Write your poems on other paper appropriate for display.

Limericks

The **limerick** is an old French and English form. It is a light or humorous verse with five chiefly anapestic (˘˘´) lines. (See the student handout, Rhythm and Meter, on page 11.) Lines 1, 2, and 5 have three feet and lines 3 and 4 have two feet. The rhyme scheme is *aabba.* License is often taken with the rules of a limerick, often with hilarious results.

EXAMPLE:

MOUSE IN HER ROOM

A mouse in her room woke Mrs. Dowd.
She was scared and she screamed very loud.
    Then a happy thought hit'r,
    To scare off the wild crit'r,
So she sat up in bed and meowed.

Anonymous

The first collections of limericks in English were published in the 1820s and by the twentieth century, they had become very popular. Contests were held to see who could give the best finish to one, two, or even four limerick lines. Complete the following limerick starter:

There was once a young girl from Macon,
Who preferred her eggs served with bacon.
    She read *Green Eggs and Ham,*
    And fell for Sam-I-Am,
____

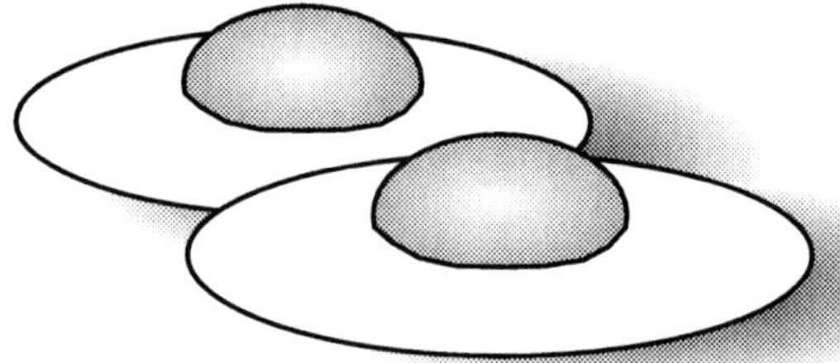

Write your own limericks. Remember, the more absurd they are, the better!

____
____
____
____
____

____
____
____
____
____

 © Educational Impressions, Inc.

Part Three:

Types of Poetry

TYPES OF POETRY

Teacher Directions

I have chosen to work with traditional poetry, free-verse poetry, narrative poetry, and lyric poetry in the student activities. Ballads, blank verse, dramatic poetry, elegies, epics, idylls, odes, sonnets, and villanelles are also described in the following teacher directions. Use them as additional activities for those students who are gifted in writing poetry and/or enjoy the challenge of working within a traditional poetry pattern.

ACTIVITY NO. 22: TRADITIONAL POETRY

Answers to the questions regarding "The Maple":
1. What kind of stanza is used in the poem?
Answer: Quatrain (See Part 2.)
2. What is the rhyme scheme?
Answer: *abcb* (See Part 4.)
3. Is the rhyme scheme the same in each stanza?
Answer: Yes (See Part 4.)
4. How many syllables are in each line?
Answer: Eight
5. How many feet are in each line? What is the primary foot used?
Answer: Four iambic (unstressed, stressed) feet are used. (See Part 1, Rhythm and Meter.)

ADDITIONAL INFORMATION:

A **rhyming free verse poem** is one that rhymes in an irregular pattern. It is not to be confused with traditional poems that rhyme in a regular pattern.

Blank verse is unrhymed poetry written in iambic (˘ ´) pentameter (five feet per line). Blank verse sounds like regular spoken English and has been used by many writers, including William Shakespeare and Robert Frost. The following is an example of blank verse:

Pindarus: So, I am free, yet would not so have been,
Durst I have done my will. O Cassius!
Far from this country Pindarus shall run,
Where never Roman shall take note of him.

William Shakespeare, *Julius Caesar,* Act V, scene iii

An **end-stopped line** ends with a pause or a full stop. It is punctuated with a comma, a dash, a semi-colon, a question mark, an exclamation point, or a period.

A **run-on line** does not have a natural pause or stop at the end of the line. The thought continues without pause into the next line. Poets use run-on lines to break the monotony of a too-regular meter and to keep the lines of a poem a manageable length.

 © Educational Impressions, Inc.

ACTIVITY NO. 23: FREE VERSE

You might like to start your poetry unit with free verse. It is the easiest kind of poetry for students to write; however, younger students usually like their poetry to rhyme.

"Mountain Stream," was written by a tenth grader after a weekend trip with her parents to the Smoky Mountains in Tennessee and North Carolina in the fall of the year.

2. The simile is "Fallen leaves, like miniature ships…"
3. The personification is "The sun flirts…kisses…and dances…"

A **prose** poem is a work that is predominantly prose but has characteristics and qualities of poetry. Martin Luther King, Jr.'s "I Have a Dream" is a well-known example.

ACTIVITY NO. 24: NARRATIVE POETRY

There are many types of narrative poetry. Ballads, epics, and metrical romances are three examples of narrative poetry.

Ballads use quatrains or sestets to recount the stories of people caught up in dramatic events. There are two types of ballads: folk ballads, such as "Barbara Allen," with unknown authorship and literary ballads, where the authorship is usually known.

Epics are long narrative poems which recount the adventures of gods and heroes. Examples are Homer's *Iliad* and *Odyssey.*

Metrical Romances present fantastic events in romantic settings involving love, honor, loyalty, and chivalry. An example is *Idylls of the King,* by Alfred, Lord Tennyson.

Additional narrative poems you might like to use with your students include the following: *The Highwayman,* by Alfred Noyes; *Lord Randal,* author unknown; and *Skeleton in Armor,* by Henry Wadsworth Longfellow.

ACTIVITY NO. 25: LYRIC POETRY

The majority of poetry is **lyric poetry.** Younger students usually like narrative poetry, such as that of Dr. Seuss, more than lyric poetry, but as students get older, they start liking lyric poetry also, especially if it strikes a cord with them. Although middle-school students still like their poems to rhyme, the middle grades are probably a good time to get students involved with writing free-verse lyric poetry as well.

You might like to suggest topics when students are having difficulty thinking of something to write about. You might make a grab-bag of ideas; students blindly reach in and select a topic. Also see Part 5, Getting and Developing Ideas.

OTHER TYPES OF POETRY

ELEGIES:
An **elegy** is a formal lyric poem mourning the death of someone or the passing of an age. An elegy is serious and solemn. "When Lilacs Last in the Dooryard Bloom'd," by Walt Whitman, laments the death of President Lincoln.

IDYLLS
An **idyll** is a poem that describes and idealizes country life.

ODES
An **ode** is usually written for a private occasion or a public ceremony. It may honor a person, commemorate an event, respond to a natural scene, or deal with a serious human problem. An ode is a serious, long, formal lyric poem, usually with a traditional stanza structure.

SONNETS
A **sonnet** is a fourteen-line poem. Usually sonnets are written in iambic (˘ ´) pentameter (five feet per line). Poets do vary the meter and the length of lines occasionally to avoid a sing-song quality. There are two major types of sonnets: the Petrarchan, or Italian, sonnet and the Shakespearean, or English, sonnet.

> A **Petrarchan (Italian) sonnet** is composed of an octave and a sestet. The octave rhymes *abbaabba.* The sestet rhymes *cdecde* (or some other combination of *cd* rhyme).
>
> A **Shakespearean (English) sonnet** has three quatrains that rhyme *abab cdcd efef* and a concluding rhyming couplet that rhymes *gg.*

EXAMPLE OF A SHAKESPEAREAN (ENGLISH) SONNET:

THE MIGHTY MAPLE

The mighty maple is a shelt'ring tree,
Its leafy, shading branches spreading wide,
Where singing birds can build nests, high and free,
And playful squirrels can find a place to hide.

A table set with ice-cold lemonade,
Two weathered rocking chairs and old oak swing
Invite us all to share its leafy shade,
And sit and listen to the song birds sing.

Its leaves are burnished silver in the spring,
A deep emerald green in summer time,
Golden on autumn days as birds take wing,
Leaving its branches bare in winter time.

The mighty maple is a shelt'ring tree.
It offers its shelter completely free.

 © Educational Impressions, Inc.

VILLANELLES

A **villanelle** is a popular type of French poetry. It is a nineteen-line poem that adheres to a strict pattern. It has five tercets that all rhyme *aba* and a concluding quatrain that rhymes *abaa.* The poem has only two rhymes. Lines 1, 6, 12, and 18 repeat and lines 3, 9, 15, and 19 repeat to form two interlocking refrains.

EXAMPLE OF A VILLANELLE:

See Part 4, Activity No. 28 for an explanation of approximate rhyme (*do* and *grow, true* and *do,* and *go* and *do.*)

EVERYTHING I GROW

I grow by doing what I have to do;
I grow by loving those who are most dear;
I feed my soul with everything I grow.

I teach myself to learn what I must know;
I grow by facing daunting, crippling fear;
I grow by doing what I have to do.

I grow as I listen and as I know;
Assimilating truth must be sincere;
I feed my soul with everything I grow.

I search for that which is forever true;
Eventually an open path comes clear;
I grow by doing what I have to do.

I see and listen everywhere I go;
I grow as I listen to what I need to hear;
I feed my soul with everything I grow.

I grow a little everywhere I go,
Understanding my soul is a last frontier.
I grow by doing what I have to do;
I feed my soul with everything I grow.

CONFESSIONAL POETRY

Confessional poetry tells of personal matters, often with extreme candor. Sylvia Plath is an example of a confessional poet.

DRAMATIC POETRY

Dramatic poetry has one or more speakers. In a **dramatic monologue** only one character speaks. In a **dramatic dialogue** two or more characters speak. The speakers in dramatic poetry speak directly. Dramatic poems resemble mini-plays and often include elements of narrative, such as setting, conflict, and plot, in addition to characters. Dramatic poetry may be traditional in form or it may be free verse.

© Educational Impressions, Inc.

EXAMPLE OF DRAMATIC POETRY:

"MOM, CAN I KEEP HIM?"

"Mom, can I keep him?
He followed me home.
Can I keep him, please, please, please?"

"Danny, don't be such a little tease.
You know that nothing followed you home."

"Oh, yes he did, Mom.
He looks like he might be a Chinese Hercules.
Can I keep him, please, please, please?"

"Danny, where is this Chinese Hercules?"

"O.K., Mom, maybe he's Hermes or Pericles.
Or maybe even Ulysses.
He's one of those heroes or gods,
Just look at him. He's about to sneeze.
Can't we get him out of this breeze?
Can I keep him, please, please, please?"

"Danny, where is this Chinese Hercules?
Or is he Hermes, or Pericles, or even Ulysses?"

"Mom, he's about to freeze.
Let's get him out of this breeze.
Can't you hear him sneeze, sneeze, sneeze—
Oh, Mom, now he's displeased.
You didn't make him welcome.
You didn't make him feel at ease,
But still, can I keep him, please, please, please?"

"No, Danny, you can't.
It's time to put your book away.
Turn out the light and go to sleep."

"O.K, Mom, I'll just hug you with a squeeze.
Goodnight, Mom. She's gone now, Chinese Hercules.
I'll get my flashlight and book,
And we'll be on our way
To save Persephone from Hades.
Won't you come with me, please, please, please?"

 © Educational Impressions, Inc.

Traditional Poetry

Traditional poetry is divided into lines and stanzas. It has regular rhythmical patterns, or meter, and a definite rhyme scheme.

EXAMPLE:

THE MAPLE

The maple is a shelt'ring tree,
Its leafy branches spreading wide,
Where singing birds can build their nests,
And squirrels can find a place to hide.

Its leaves are silver in the spring,
But they turn golden in the fall.
It throws wide shadows on the grass,
Where children toss and catch their ball.

A swing entices from a limb,
A knotted climbing rope nearby.
In evening breeze its branches fan
And sing a cooling lullaby.

A table with weathered benches,
A pitcher of cold lemonade,
Two rocking chairs with peeling paint
Invite all to its shelt'ring shade.

The maple is a shelt'ring tree,
Its leafy branches spreading wide.
It shelters all who come to it
And does it with abiding pride.

1. What kind of stanza is used in the poem?

____

2. What is the rhyme scheme?

____

3. Is the rhyme scheme the same in each stanza?

____

4. How many syllables are in each line?

____

5. How many feet are in each line? What is the primary foot used?

____

Free Verse

Free verse has no regular pattern of rhythm and rhyme. Stanzas, if they are used, may vary in number of lines, and the lines themselves may be of varying length. Many poetic elements, such as figurative language and repetition, may be used. Rhythm and rhyme may also occur, but not as part of a regular pattern. Instead of following a set metrical pattern, a poem in free verse could have a rhythm which echoes its meaning.

Free verse may sound more like prose than poetry because the verse lines are more akin to prose sentences. The free-verse poet's use of line breaks and placement on the page indicate that the composition is poetry. Remember, when you write free verse, let the words you use to express your moods, ideas, perceptions, or feelings take their own natural form.

EXAMPLE:

MOUNTAIN STREAM

Miniature waterfalls
        Cascade
        into
Ice cold pools below.
Stereophonic water
        Rushes in cadence
        Over the rocks,
Worn lustrous through eternity.
Fallen leaves, like miniature ships,
Sail silently, moving with the unrelenting current.
The sun flirts through the trees,
Kisses the shimmering pools,
And dances away over the water.
Autumn trees waver from the depths of the water,
Reflecting God's handiwork.

Linda Bowman, Grade 10

1. How do the word choices (diction) help you visualize the scene described in the poem?

____

2. What is the simile in the poem? How effective is it?

____

3. What is the personification in the poem?

____

4. What is the effect of the arrangement of the lines?

____

5. In the last line, could "Nature's" be an alternate word choice for "God's"? Why or why not?

____

 © Educational Impressions, Inc.

Free Verse

Create your own free-verse poem. Before you begin, think about the following questions:

- What will be the subject of your poem?
- What are some of your feelings about the subject?
- What are some of your ideas about the subject?
- What mood will you want to create?
- What types of figurative language will you use to help you create that mood?
- Will you use repetition to help you create that mood?

© Educational Impressions, Inc.

Narrative Poetry

A **narrative poem** tells a story. Narrative poetry can be humorous or serious; rhymed or unrhymed; traditional in form, blank verse, or free verse. Its only requirement is that it tell a story.

EXAMPLE:

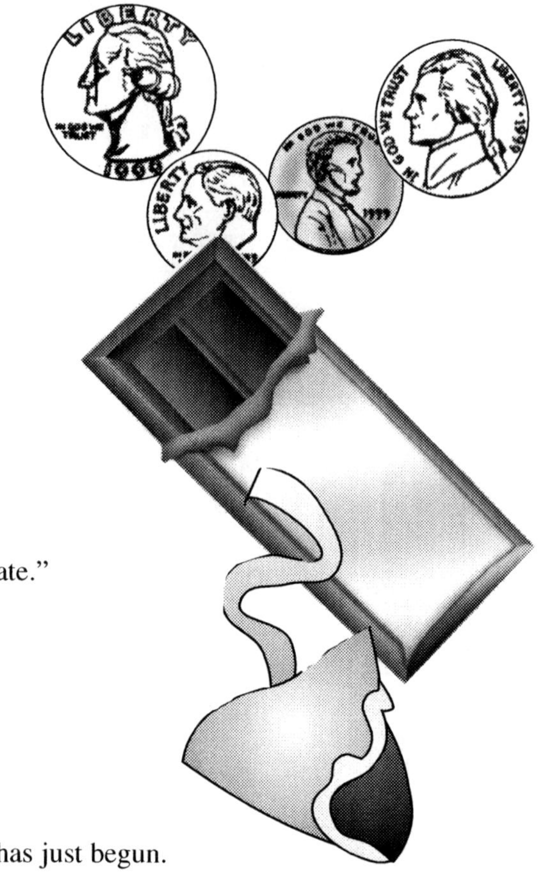

BLACK JACK JENKINS

Black Jack Jenkins was a flim-flam man.
He caused pandemonium all over the land.
He conned fuddy-duddies out of their hard-earned money,
Then used it to live a life of milk and honey.

He also liked to work a Plain Jane target,
With whom he could make a very quick profit.
He'd tempt her with a chocolate sweet-treat,
Then steal her cash—leave her standing in the street.

One unhappy day he collided with his fate.
Elaine the Brain, sister of Plain Jane, whispered, "Checkmate."
She turned the tables, beat him at his own game.
Now Black Jack Jenkins has a number for a name.

While Elaine the Brain, sister of Plain Jane,
Is happily enjoying her unexpected fame.
She's a regular on TV, a media darling "must see,"
And her book, *Checking Black Jack,* is number one,
And the filming of the movie, starring a Hollywood cutie, has just begun.

Tell a story in poetry. You might first like to write it in prose and then turn it into poetry. Conversation can be used in poetry just as it is used in prose or drama. Jot your ideas in the space below. Write your poem on another sheet of paper.

© Educational Impressions, Inc.

Lyric Poetry

Lyric poetry expresses the thoughts, emotions, feelings, and opinions of the poet through vivid words and images that help the reader picture and share the experience. The poet uses these words and images to appeal to the reader's senses of taste, touch, sight, sound, and smell. Lyric poetry does not tell a story as narrative poetry does; however, sometimes a scene is set or an action shown from which a conclusion can be drawn.

Lyric poetry may be rhymed or unrhymed.

EXAMPLES:

GOOD INTENTIONS

I intended to do my homework today,
To do my math and then be on my way,
To study the memorable Kennedy-Nixon Debate,
To bring my journal entries up to date.

But a butterfly flitted among the flowers,
And a spider's web glittered with morning dew,
While a cardinal sang in the old peach tree,
And all the leaves called out to me.

A soft breeze sighed among the trees.
A love song whispered to the buzzing bees,
Tickling the wind chimes with brief kisses
And caressing the jasmines draped over the trellises.

Then a sunbeam beckoned with a seductive smile,
Dancing across the emerald meadow with enticing guile,
Tempting—"Come and play with me for just a little while."

So what could I do but laugh and follow?
The good intentions could wait 'til the morrow.

CAT

Couched, ready to pounce,
Tail slowly twitching,
Attentive,
Slitted green eyes tracking every movement,
Tracking the prey, tracking the prey—
Stalking, stalking, stalking—

Lyric Poetry

Create a lyric poem. Use one of the ideas suggested below or one of your own.

SUGGESTED TOPICS

A summer (autumn, winter, spring) day

The first spring flower (specify)

A basketball game

A baseball game

A hockey game

The half-time performance of the band

The sounds of any holiday

The tastes of any holiday

A Saturday afternoon at the mall

The first snowfall of the year

A football game

A soccer game

Cheerleaders at one of the above

An animal

The sights of any holiday

The smells of any holiday

 © Educational Impressions, Inc.

Part Four:

Elements of Poetry

ELEMENTS OF POETRY

Teacher Directions

ACTIVITY NO. 26: FIGURATIVE LANGUAGE
This activity contains an overview of figurative language. Discuss its importance in poetry.

ACTIVITY NO. 26 A: SIMILES
You might like to group students into small groups to work on similes. Using some of the brainstorming techniques can sometimes help students generate more ideas.

ACTIVITY NO. 26 B: METAPHORS
Use the same group techniques with metaphors that you used with similes. Students can change similes to metaphors and vice versa. As an example, have them add *like* to the first line of either or both sample poems. Ask students if and how this changes the meaning or intensity.

Discuss mixed metaphors and dead metaphors. A **mixed metaphor** happens when two or more metaphors are mixed together. For instance, "water under the bridge" and "evening of life" might be mixed as "evening under the bridge." Metaphors, under normal circumstances, should not be mixed. However, some writers intentionally mix metaphors for humorous effects. A **dead metaphor** is one that has been used so long and so often that we no longer think of it as a metaphor, such as the arm of a chair.

ACTIVITY NO. 26 C and D: UNDERSTATEMENT and OVERSTATEMENT
The following are possible understatements:

a tornado: a little whirlwind
a hurricane: a soft breeze
a Mercedes: a toy car
the Hope Diamond: a little stone

The following are possible overstatements:

a headache: an atom bomb explosion
a vacation: Dante's Inferno (bad)
Paradise on a cloud (good)
a misunderstanding with a friend: World War II
a meal: last meal of a condemned man (bad)
Thanksgiving & Christmas in 1 (good)

ACTIVITY NOS. 26 E and F: OXYMORA AND PARADOXES
There are websites for oxymora. You might like to look at some for additional examples. Most will be connected with current events.

ACTIVITY NO. 26 G and H PERSONIFICATION AND APOSTROPHE
Have students choose one or more of the following and give them human characteristics: desk, shoes, bicycle, telephone, pencil, lunch box, window blinds, swimming pool, and front doors of school.

ACTIVITY NO. 26 I: OTHER FIGURES OF SPEECH
Depending on the level of your class and your time limits, you might not want to include all the figures of speech. Try to include symbol and allusion.

 © Educational Impressions, Inc.

Have students make a list of common symbols, such as flags and mascots. Don't forget to talk about words, both oral and written, as symbols.

In "The pen is mightier than the sword," *pen* suggests written words and *sword* represents armies or fighting.

The irony in "The Altercation" is that Jim bit the dog.

Discuss the importance of allusions in poetry. Mythology, history, literature, the Bible, politics, current events, and popular culture are sources for allusions.

ACTIVITY NO. 26 J–L: FUN WITH FIGURES OF SPEECH (K, Clichés)

The following clichés are similes: cold as ice, snug as a bug in a rug, fresh as the morning dew, fresh as a daisy, dead as a doornail, old as the hills, spread like wildfire, and timid as a mouse.

ACTIVITY NO. 27: APPEALS TO THE SENSES, SENSORY LANGUAGE

The following are answers to the questions about "First Peach":

1. Fluted "Birdy! Birdy! Birdy!"
2. Fragrance of ripe peaches
3. Luscious juice
4. Plucked, weighed...hand, rubbed...cheek, down...chin
5. Gnarled peach trees, concealing rock wall, pendulous...fruit, scarlet flash, overreaching limb, golden rose orb, palm of my hand, rubbed...against my cheek, spurted, ran down my chin
6. Strolled, flash, lit, reaching out, plucked, weighed, rubbed, spurted, ran down

ACTIVITY NO. 27 A: APPEALS TO THE SENSES, ONOMATOPOEIA

The onomatopoetic words are: murmur, sighing, hum, moan, snarling, scream, cracking, booming, drummed, beating, hammered, crashed, slammed, banged, whisper, dripped, and plopping.

ADDITIONAL INFORMATION ABOUT THE WAY THINGS SOUND TO US:
Euphony: agreeable sound, especially in the spoken quality of words
Euphonious: pleasing or agreeable to the ear; harmonious; musical
Cacophony: jarring, discordant sound; the harsh or unharmonious use of language
Cacophonous: having a harsh, unpleasant sound

ACTIVITY NO. 28 A–D: REPETITION AND RHYME

Readers, especially young ones, expect a pattern in poetry and enjoy recognizing that pattern. The pattern in "Retreat" is *abcb.*

The following are answers to the questions about "The Altercation" in Activity No. 28 A:

1. Altercation, provocation; pen, chin, Jim; meditation, retaliation, mediation, negotiation, conciliation; agree, me; eye, me; hat, that; grin, chin
2. Line 8: took, notebook
   Line 9: pen, chin (approximate rhyme)
3. Lines 5 and 6: hat, throat
   Lines 8 and 9: pen, chin
   Lines 9 and 10: chin, Jim
   Lines 21 and 22: eye, me

The following poem could be created from the three lines beginning "She saw the fine sign."

BON-BON'S CREATION

Bon-Bon saw the fine sign
Advertising a Hodge-Podge Flower Shower Day,
On Saturday, the fifth day of May.
She planted her sassafras tree
In that old discarded Hot-Pot,
Then used her crayons to color it in shades of blue,
Including robin's egg and forget-me-not,
And entered it in the contest
To see if it would win or not.
The fuddy-duddy judges said, "O-o-o-oh!"
And then they sighed, "Ah-h-h-h,"
As they placed a cerulean blue ribbon
On Bon-Bon's sassafras-Hot-Pot-and-crayon creation.

OPTIONS:

1. Have students rhyme their names, such as Blue-Eyed Clyde, Together Heather, Brainy Janey, and Neat Keith. (See Activity No. 28 A, Repetition and Rhyme, for different kinds of rhyme.)

2. Have students compile a list of words ending in "-ation." Then have them use them in rhyming couplets, triplets, or quatrains. A partial list follows:

Creation	Radiation	Mediation	Recreation
Fascination	Retaliation	Association	Explanation
Inauguration	Appreciation	Aviation	Negotiation
Affiliation	Humiliation	Conciliation	Identification
Location	Vocation	Vacation	Altercation
Provocation	Variation	Education	Renovation
Conservation	Reservation	Observation	Plantation
Vibration	Incubation	Contemplation	Designation
Expectation	Consultation	Graduation	Situation

Note of interest: There are no exact rhymes for silver, orange, purple, or month.

The following are answers to the questions about "The Altercation":
1. Alliteration is used in lines 7, 14, 21, and 28.
2. The alliterative words are **b**loody and **b**lack; **b**arked and **b**ack; **b**loody and **b**lack; and **d**og, **d**irty, and **d**oggy.

The following are a few of the many examples of assonance in "The Altercation":
Line 1: "Th**e** **ALLEGED** **al**t**e**rc**a**tion," (a, e)
Line 7: L**oo**ked **a**t Jim's bl**oo**dy n**o**se and bl**a**ck eye, (o, a)
Line 12: Right here **o**n my **o**wn fr**o**nt p**o**rch, (o)

The following are examples of consonance in "The Altercation":
Lines 5 and 23: rese**t** and ha**t** (t)
Line 28: bi**t** and tha**t** (t)
Line 24: bac**k** and nec**k** (k)

© **Educational Impressions, Inc.**

ADDITIONAL INFORMATION

You might want to discuss the following concepts with your students:

POETIC LICENSE

Poetic license is the liberty taken, especially by an artist or writer, in deviating from conventional form or fact to achieve a desired effect. Poetic license is taken in all forms of writing—poetry, prose, and drama. It is used for humorous effects, to condense and compress events and time, for emotional effects, to create suspense, to dramatize, and to heighten awareness.

RHYTHM AND METER

See the student handout on page 11. With younger students, you may choose to discuss rhythm and meter in general terms as opposed to the in-depth listing of feet and lines that I have included. I sometimes find it helpful to use a "bing-bong" method when talking about poetic feet. I use "bing" for unstressed syllables and "bong" for stressed syllables. Thus, an iambic foot would be "bing-bong," and a trochaic foot would be "bong-bing." This method has been very successful for me.

DENOTATION AND CONNOTATION

Denotation is the literal meaning, the dictionary definition, of a word.

Connotation includes the literal meaning of the word plus all associated and emotional meanings of the word. Which would you rather buy, an antique chest or an old bureau? Poets make frequent use of words rich in connotations to appeal to the emotions and to expand the reach of words.

Figurative Language

Figurative language is not meant to be interpreted literally. Poets use figures of speech to express ideas boldly and imaginatively. **Figures of speech** serve several functions in poetry:

- Figures of speech give us imaginative pleasure. The mind delights in the leaps needed for making connections and in seeing similarities between two things that are normally unlike each other.
- Figures of speech help make abstract ideas concrete; they call for the use of all five senses.
- Figures of speech convey attitudes with information and add emotional depth to otherwise informative statements.
- Figures of speech are concentrated; they say more with fewer words.
- Figures of speech add a richness, an extra layer of meaning, to poetry.

Many kinds of figures of speech are used by poets, including the following:

Simile	Metaphor	Personification	Paradox
Understatement	Hyperbole	Oxymoron	Apostrophe
Metonymy	Synechdoche	Irony	Symbolism

NOTE: Allusion is not generally included as a figure of speech; however, because it is used to make a comparison, it has been included in this section.

With which of the above figures of speech are you familiar?

____

____

____

Which of the above figures of speech are new to you?

____

____

____

 © Educational Impressions, Inc.

Similes

A **simile** is a figure of speech that uses *like, as, than, similar to, resembles, seems,* or a similar word or phrase to make a direct comparison between two unlike things. Poets use similes to help readers make connections.

EXAMPLES OF SIMILES:

My love is like a red, red rose.

Her eyes were as green as Irish hills.

His jealousy was as green as a St. Patrick's Day flag.

Her mood was as brown as autumn.

His fury was as red as Valentine hearts.

THE MOON

Like a baby peeping
Over the side of her crib,
The moon stood on tiptoe
To peer over the far hills.

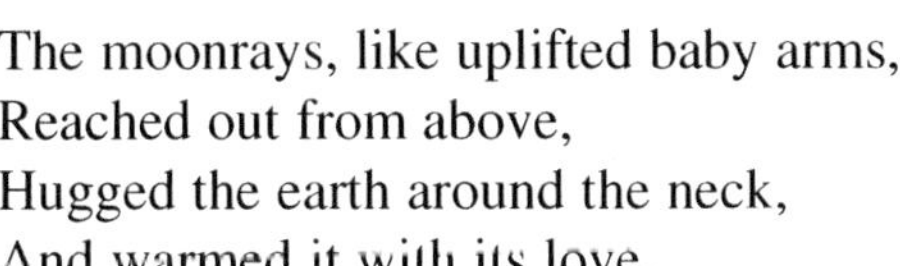

The moonrays, like uplifted baby arms,
Reached out from above,
Hugged the earth around the neck,
And warmed it with its love.

Complete the following similes:

Rare as ____________________ Pretty as ____________________

Jealous as ____________________ Anger like ____________________

Tiny as ____________________ Intelligent as ____________________

Funny like ____________________ Sticky like ____________________

Clear as ____________________ Shy as ____________________

Choose one or more of your completed similes (or supply one of your own) and create a poem. The poem can be free verse or traditional. Use another sheet of paper if necessary.

____

____

____

____

____

____

Metaphors

Like a simile, a **metaphor** is also also a figure of speech that compares two unlike things. One thing is spoken of as if it were another, suggesting comparison. Usually, a form of *is* or another "being" verb is used to make the comparison. Metaphors may also be written as appositives.

EXAMPLES OF METAPHORS:

Death is a long sleep. (Death, the long sleep…)
Life is a braying hound. (Life, the braying hound…)
You are a big ape. (You big ape…)
She has an eagle eye.
He was treason in a blue suit.

An **extended metaphor** is a metaphor which is developed through several lines of a poem. Sometimes, as in the following example, it is the whole poem.

NATURE'S CHILD

She is a ruby-throated hummingbird,
Flying with natural precision,
Without fanfare,
From elsewhere to somewhere,
Sipping a little here,
Taking just a taste there,
For her continued welfare—
Only her fair share.

Complete the following metaphors and add three of your own:

A sneeze is ____________________

Final exams are ____________________

Summer vacation is ____________________

Broccoli is ____________________

____

____

____

 © Educational Impressions, Inc.

Metaphors

Like the poem on the previous page, this poem is an example of an **extended metaphor.**

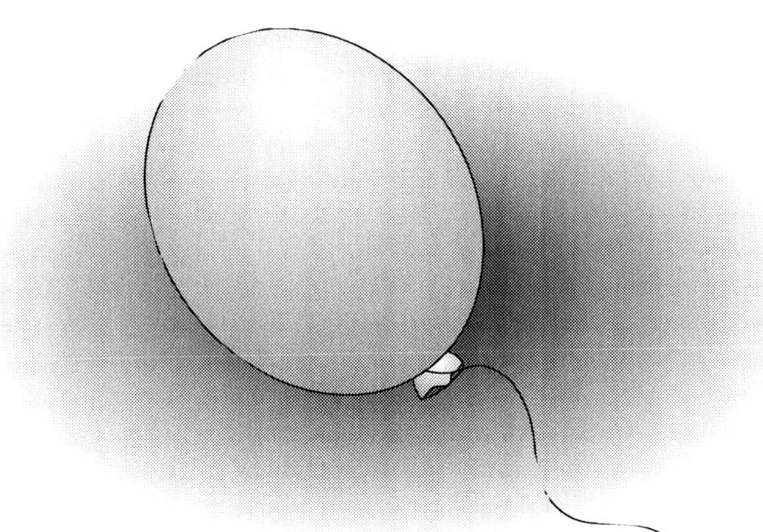

THE BALLOON

The ego is a balloon
Of great elasticity.
It can be inflated
And float
Above the clouds,
Until a gusty wind
Sweeps it to
The jagged terrain.
Upon contact with
Reality, it bursts—
A membrane,
Forever deflated.

Debra Newell, Grade 10

Create your own extended metaphor. It may or may not be your entire poem.

Understatement

Understatements can be humorous or serious, restrained or fanciful, and convincing or unconvincing. Poets use understatement for humorous effect or to emphasize the truth.

An **understatement** says less than is meant, often in an ironic way.

EXAMPLES OF UNDERSTATEMENT:
Calling a…

- downpour a "sprinkle"
- roaring lion a "purring kitten"
- Mt. Everest a "little hill"
- banquet a "quick snack"
- castle "that shack on the hill"

VISITING

While visiting the American White House,
That little cottage in Washington, D.C.,
Mary Strauss told Marty, her spouse,
"It would take a presidential decree
To get me to clean that house
With nothing but a broom, a bucket, and a squeegee."

Write a sentence for each using understatement:

A tornado: ______________________________

A Mercedes: ______________________________

A hurricane: ______________________________

The Hope Diamond: ______________________________

Use an understatement above or one of your own and write a short poem, rhymed or unrhymed.

____

____

____

____

____

____

 © Educational Impressions, Inc.

Overstatement

An **overstatement,** or **hyperbole,** is ia deliberate exaggeration. Like understatements, overstatements can be humorous or serious, restrained or fanciful, and convincing or unconvincing.

EXAMPLES OF OVERSTATEMENT:
Calling a…
mild-mannered kitten a "roaring lion"
drizzle a "cloudburst"
pimple on the nose "Mt. Everest"

JUMPING JIM JOINER

Jumping Jim Joiner
Can't be beat.
Doesn't need air cushions,
Has springs in his feet.

Can that boy jump?
You bet he can!
See that man in the moon?
Jumping Jim shakes his hand.

Write a sentence for each using overstatement:

A headache: ______________________

A vacation: ______________________

A meal: ______________________

A misunderstanding with a friend: ______________________

Use an overstatement above or one of your own and write a short poem, rhymed or unrhymed.

© Educational Impressions, Inc.

Oxymora

An **oxymoron** is a figure of speech which combines contradictory, incongruous, or opposing ideas. Oxymora are used by poets to suggest paradoxes in a few words.

EXAMPLES OF OXYMORA:

Cruel kindness
Bitterly happy
Open secret
Beautifully ugly
Mercy killing
Mournful optimist

Burning cold
Idiotic wisdom
Benign menace
Sweet sorrow
Living dead
Freezing fire

Add your own oxymora to the above list. Use one or more of the oxymora to write a poem, rhymed or unrhymed.

 © Educational Impressions, Inc.

Paradoxes

A **paradox** is a figure of speech that on the surface seems to be contradictory, but upon closer examination actually presents a truth. Poets use paradoxes to surprise and shock readers and to draw their attention and deeper thoughts to what is said.

EXAMPLES OF PARADOXES:

Success won't come to me unless I go to it.

Your fire is freezing me.

"I am old and young, of the foolish as much as the wise."—*Walt Whitman*

"Much madness is divinest sense…much sense the starkest madness."—*Emily Dickinson*

Add two of your own paradoxes to the examples above.

Use a paradox as the basis of a poem. You might like to use one of the following poem-starters:

He/she was the laziest busy person I ever knew.

She wasn't very pretty, but she was gorgeous to me.

He/she was the tallest short person I ever met, a little giant.

© Educational Impressions, Inc.

Personification

A **personification** is the giving of a human quality to an inanimate object or a concept. Poets use personification to make things or ideas seem alive and vibrant. Personification is actually a sub-type of metaphor because there is an implied comparison to humans. (See "The Moon" in Activity No. 26 A.)

EXAMPLES OF PERSONIFICATION:

Let the sun kiss your cheeks.

The wind will whisper his secrets to you.

The morning dew will bathe your sorrows.

Add your own examples to the above list.

Write a poem using personification. Use one of the examples above or create one of your own.

SUNSET

The sun grows drowsy,
The brilliance of its rays
Bathing the land in a golden glow.
A flood of orange and pink
Pours across the darkening sky.
Night turns back the covers,
And the eye of the heavens retires.

Donna Workman, Grade 12

 © Educational Impressions, Inc.

Apostrophe

An **apostrophe** is an address to an absent person, a dead person, or a personified object or idea. It is usually used to add emotional depth to a poem.

EXAMPLES OF APOSTROPHE:

Oh, Moon…
Dear Christmas Eve, how eagerly we awaited your arrival…

Write three sentences using apostrophe.

____

____

____

____

The following poem has examples of personification and apostrophe:

Dear Sunshine,
Shine on my sorrows.
Dry them up so that
The Welcome Wind
Can blow them away.

Write a poem using apostrophe. Use one of the examples above or create one of your own.

© Educational Impressions, Inc.

Other Figures of Speech and Allusion

Symbolism is the use of something to stand for, or represent, something else. Poets use symbols to enrich their poems and to add deeper levels of meaning to their poems. A robin might be used as a symbol of spring. A road or a river might represent the journey of life.

Name six common symbols. Don't forget that words, too, can be important symbols.

______________________ ______________________ ______________________

______________________ ______________________ ______________________

Metonymy is a figure of speech in which an attribute of something is used to suggest that thing. "Crown" might be used to suggest "monarch."

Explain the two examples of metonymy in the following sentence: The pen is mightier than the sword.

____

____

Synechdoche is a figure of speech in which a part stands for the whole or the whole for a part. "Hand" may be used to represent worker. "Mouths" may be used to represent people. "Start the car" actually means start the engine.

Write a sentence using synechdoche.

____

____

Irony is the general term given to literary techniques that involve humorous or surprising contradictions. Poets use irony to show a contrast between what is stated and what is meant or between what is expected to happen and what does happen.

Read "The Altercation" in Activity No. 28 A. What is the irony in the poem?

____

An **allusion**, which is not really a figure of speech, is an indirect reference. In poetry, it is the reference to a well-known event, person, place, literary character or work, or work of art. Poets use allusions as a shortcut to briefly suggest specific ideas or to make comparisons.

Mythology, history, literature, the Bible, politics, current events, and popular culture are sources for allusions. Find an example of allusion in literature.

 © Educational Impressions, Inc.

Fun with Figures of Speech: Idioms

RED-HANDED

I've caught you red-handed
With your hand in the cookie jar.
No need to cry over spilt milk
Or to fly off the handle
Because it's crystal clear,
You've got egg all over your face.
Now, you must face the music
For going hog wild.
You might as well keep your shirt on
Because you'll be in the doghouse for a while.

IDIOMS

The following common expressions are known as **idioms.** The literal meanings of idioms are quite different from their accepted meanings! (Of course, some may also be used literally.)

Drop me a line
Heavy foot
Heavy handed
Give me a hand
Green thumb
Hold on to your hat
Hold your horses
Keep your eye on
Put your foot down

Left holding the bag
On pins and needles
On the firing line
Pull up stakes
Pull self up by boot straps
Pull up your socks
Put a flea in her/his ear
Put a spring in your step
Keep your hands off

Scarce as hen's teeth
Selling like hot cakes
Bee in his/her bonnet
He/she has a broken heart
Talk a blue streak
Throw in the towel
Throw your hat in the ring
Keep your eyes peeled
Raining cats and dogs

Add your own idioms to the above list.

Write a poem using as many idiomatic expressions as you can.

© Educational Impressions, Inc.

Fun with Figures of Speech: Clichés

A REAL GO-GETTER

He wanted to be a real go-getter—
A home-run hitter.
He tried to keep his finger in every pie,
But as regular as clockwork,
He missed the boat.
He tried to appear cool as a cucumber,
But he was always on pins and needles,
Afraid he would appear dull as dishwater
Or weak as water.
It was clear as crystal to him
That he was quick as lightning
And straight as an arrow.
And although he was busy as a bee,
He was never quite on the cutting edge.
He wanted to be tough as nails—
Or was it old boots?
But to his everlasting sorrow,
He'd have to think about it tomorrow.

CLICHÉS

A **cliché** is an expression that has been used so often that it has become dull and almost meaningless and is now lacking originality. Most of the thousands of clichés in the English language are figures of speech. Some are examples of overstatement or understatement. Many are similes or metaphors. Some clichés are used so often that they become part of the way we say things because they offer ready-made expressions and comparisons.

The following are some common clichés:

Snug as a bug in a rug	Fresh as the morning dew	Fresh as a daisy
Dead as a doornail	Beat a dead horse	That horse won't run
That dog won't hunt	Vicious circle (cycle)	Old as the hills
Spread like wildfire	Timid as a mouse	Sneaking suspicion
______________	______________	______________
______________	______________	______________
______________	______________	______________

Add your own clichés to the list. Put a check next to those clichés which are also similes.

Use as many of the above expressions as you can in a poem. Don't forget those you added plus those in the poem "A Real Go-Getter."

 © Educational Impressions, Inc.

Fun with Figures of Speech: Aphorisms

An **aphorism** is an observation or general truth about life. Aphorisms, often witty and wise, are usually stated concisely, even tersely. Used in a poem, an original aphorism can be effective in summarizing or reinforcing a point or argument.

EXAMPLES:

From endings beginnings grow.
It's always darkest just before the dawn.
Every cloud has a silver lining.
As one door closes, another opens.
As the twig is bent, so it grows.
The fruit doesn't fall far from the tree.
The early bird gets the worm.

____

____

____

Add other aphorisms to the list.

IS THE GRASS GREENER?

I've heard all my life
That the grass is greener on the other side of the fence.
And why is it, do you suppose,
That humankind is so discontent
That we hang ourselves
Because of some vague, undefined needs,
Sticking our heads through the fence,
Just to nibble that grass on the other side
That grows from the same seeds?

Use one of the aphorisms listed above to create a quatrain.

© Educational Impressions, Inc.

Appeals to the Senses: Sensory Language

Sensory language is used by poets to appeal to one or more of the five senses: sight, sound, touch, taste, and smell.

Imagery is the descriptive or figurative language used by poets to create word pictures, or images. Poets create images by describing sight, touch, sound, smell, taste, and movement.

FIRST PEACH

I strolled past the gnarled peach tree,
Leaning toward the sun over the concealing rock wall.
Pendulous ripe fruit weighed heavy from its branches.
A scarlet flash, a fluted "Birdy! Birdy! Birdy!"
And a cardinal lit on an overreaching limb.
The fragrance of ripe peaches assaulted the air.
Tempting, Tempting—
Reaching out I plucked a golden rose orb,
Weighed its ripe weight in the palm of my hand,
And rubbed the peach down against my cheek.
The first bite spurted luscious juice,
Which ran down my chin.

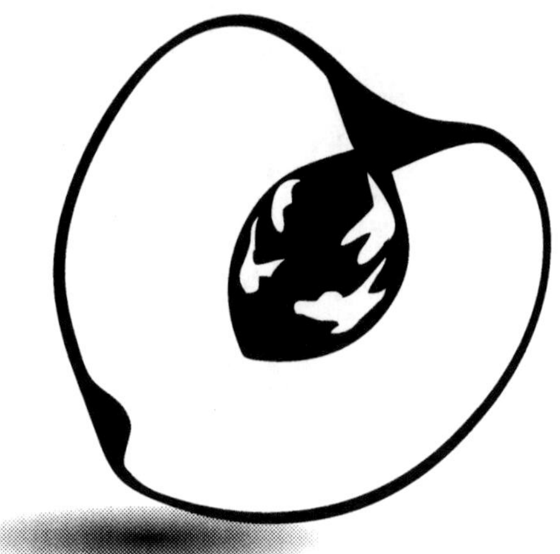

1. Which words or phrases describe sounds?

____

2. Which words or phrases describe smells?

____

3. Which words or phrases describe tastes?

____

4. Which words or phrases describe touch?

____

5. Which words or phrases describe sights?

____

6. Which words or phrases describe movement?

____

 © Educational Impressions, Inc.

Appeals to the Senses: Sensory Language

Describe one of the following suggested topics or one of your own in a sensory poem. Be as vivid and imaginative as possible. Try to include at least one simile or metaphor.

Baseball game or other athletic event
A trip to the circus
Fourth of July celebration
Another holiday celebration
Watermelon or ice cream on a hot August day
Visit to an animal shelter
First strawberries in spring
Visit to a Fall Festival
Visit to the library
Visit to a park or playground

Ask yourself the following questions as you compose your poem to help you make your readers see, smell, hear, touch, and taste your poem:

How does everything look?
How do things smell?
What are the sounds?
How do things taste?
What are the textures, the feel of things?
What are the movements, the actions?

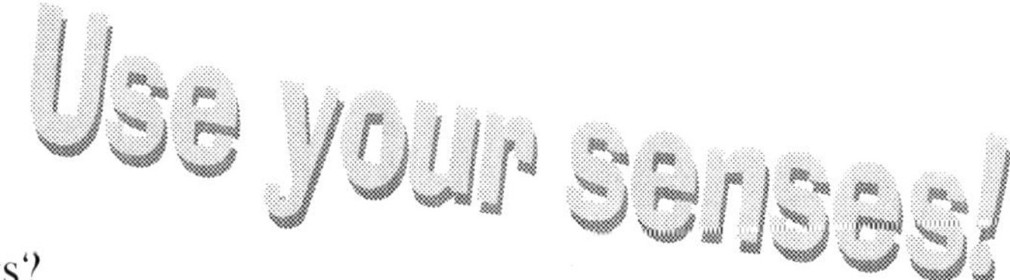

Create a poem using sensory language and imagery.

Appeals to the Senses: Onomatopoeia

Onomatopoeia occurs when the sound of a word echoes its sense. It is the use of words that imitate sounds. In poetry, onomatopoeia is used to create musical effects and to emphasize or reinforce meaning.

EXAMPLES:

bang	batter	bow-wow	buzz	drip	drum	hiss
hum	meow	moan	murmur	ooze	pow	rustle
sigh	snap	snarl	sob	splat	tick-tock	moo

SUMMER STORM

The wind began as a teasing murmur,
Sighing lightly through the trees,
Accompanied by the gentle hum of soft rain.
Too soon the wind became a moan,
Swiftly progressing to a belligerent snarling scream.
Lightning zig-zagged across the starless sky,
Briefly illuminating the face of the black night,
Followed, before the count of one, by cracking, booming thunder.
The rain drummed, beating down in penetrating sheets.
Unsecured shutters hammered, crashed, slammed, banged.
The sharp odor of ozone permeated the cooling air.
Gradually the lightning drifted east,
Followed by the diminishing crescendo of thunder.
The wind dwindled to a whisper.
Raindrops dripped softly from eaves and trees,
Plopping in iambic pentameter against the rock wall.
Her room now agleam with slanting moonbeams,
She closed her eyes
And slipped into supremely peaceful sweet dreams.

What are the onomatopoetic words in "Summer Storm"?______________________________

____

____

Write a poem using onomatopoeia. The following are some ideas to include in your poem if you wish. As you write your poem, think about the following: Can you hear your poem as you write it? Will your readers be able to hear it as they read it?

Fingernails on a chalk board
Children playing
Gym class
Snow blowers (or any tool)
Ball games (be specific)

 © Educational Impressions, Inc.

Repetition and Rhyme

Repetition is the use, two or more times, of a poetic element—a sound, a word, a phrase, a clause, a sentence, a rhythmical pattern, or a grammatical construction. Alliteration, assonance, consonance, parallelism, rhyme, rhythm, and refrains are types of repetition used in poetry.

A **refrain** is a regularly repeated line or group of lines in a poem, often at the ends of stanzas. Sometimes the whole stanza forms a refrain. In songs, a refrain is often called a chorus.

Parallelism (parallel construction) occurs when a sentence pattern or grammatical construction is repeated. It is used in poetry to link related ideas and to emphasize certain elements. (Note the parallel construction in the previous sentence: "to link related ideas" and "to emphasize certain elements." Both phrases are composed of an infinitive, an adjective, and a noun.)

Rhyme is the repetition of the same—or almost the same—sounds at the end of two or more words.

Exact Rhyme occurs when the rhyming sounds are identical. Examples of exact rhyme are love-above-dove-shove; phone-tone; and grin-chin.

Approximate Rhyme (also called slant rhyme, imperfect rhyme, near rhyme, and oblique rhyme) occurs when the sounds are similar. Examples of approximate rhyme are prove-glove and arrayed-said.

End Rhyme occurs when the ending sounds at the end of two or more lines are the same or very similar.

Internal Rhyme occurs when one or more words within a line rhyme with the ending word in that line: "While Elaine the Brain, sister of Plain Jane."

Masculine Rhyme (single rhyme) occurs when the rhyme is only in the last syllable of the rhyming words. Examples are chance-dance-enhance; bold-scold; and bald-scald.

Feminine Rhyme occurs when at least two or more syllables in words rhyme: Examples are hurrying-scurrying and ceiling-kneeling.

Traditional, or patterned, poetry follows a **rhyme scheme—**a regular pattern of rhyming words. Different letters of the alphabet at the ends of the lines are used to describe a rhyme scheme. Each new rhyme gets a new letter: *a, b, c, d,* etc.

Mark each line in the following poem with the appropriate letter to show its rhyme scheme.

RETREAT

If you don't mind, I'll stay right here ____
And hang my head over the side of my cloud. ____
I can't keep up with the rush; ____
Besides, the world talks too loud. ____

Renee Ayers, Grade 10

© Educational Impressions, Inc.

The Altercation

"The ALLEGED altercation,"
Jim told the sheriff's deputy,
"Was caused by extreme provocation."

"You don't say?"
The sheriff's deputy reset his hat,
Cleared his throat,
Looked at Jim's bloody nose and black eye,
Took out his notebook and pen,
Looked at the pen and thoughtfully scratched his chin.
"Tell me, in your own words, just what happened," he commanded Jim.

"Well, I was in the middle of my Yoga meditation,
Right here on my own front porch,
When my neighbor's Great Dane began to bark,
So, I barked back in retaliation.
Now, in hindsight, and I'm sure you'll agree,
I should have tried mediation
Or some other form of negotiation.
Obviously, the dog thought that I was another dog
Because he jumped the fence and attacked me.
By this time it was too late for conciliation."

Pointing to his bloody nose and black eye,
Jim said, "Just look at what he did to me."

The sheriff's deputy again reset his hat
And this time scratched the back of his neck.
He asked, "What happened next?
Just in your own words, please. Can you do that?"

"Well," Jim admitted, with an abashed grin,
"I bit that dog right back on his dirty little doggy chin."

Answer the following questions about "The Altercation."

1. What are the end rhymes in the poem?____________________________

2. What is the internal rhyme?____________________________

3. What are three examples of approximate, or slant, rhyme?__________________

 © Educational Impressions, Inc.

Rhyme Time

Use as many of the following rhyming word pairs in a poem as possible:

Black Jack or black jack
Bow-wow
Cha-cha
Fine sign
Flower shower
Fuddy-duddy
Heebie-jeebies
Helter-skelter
Heyday
Hodge-podge
Hot-pot or hot pot
Hum-drum
Jelly-belly
Kowtow
Nickel pickle
Oh and ah or ooh and ah
Peg leg
Pell mell
Plain Jane
Pop-top
Rag-tag
Sassafras
Sweet treat
Ting-a-ling

POEM-STARTER: Complete the following poem-starter. You may revise as necessary. Give your poem a title.

____

(Title)

She saw the fine sign
Advertising a Hodge-Podge Flower Shower Day,
On Saturday, the fifth day of May.

© Educational Impressions, Inc.

Alliteration

Alliteration is the repetition of consonant sounds at the beginning of words or accented syllables. Poets use alliteration to create musical effects in poetry.

Some names are alliterative: Marilyn Monroe and William Walton Wolfe (my grandfather!).

Most tongue twisters are composed of a series of alliterative words:

Peter Piper picked a peck of pickled peppers…
She sells sea shells by the sea shore.

Study "The Altercation," Activity 28 A. Then answer the following questions:

1. In what four lines is alliteration used in the poem? ____________________

2. What are the alliterative words? ____________________

____

Use a few of the following alliterative phrases in a quatrain. The poem can be rhymed or unrhymed.

Bing bang	Flip-flop	Lip-lap	Slip-slap
Cling clang	Gewgaw	Mish-mash	Splish-splash
Dilly-dally	He-haw	Riffraff	Topsy-turvy
Ding-dong	Ho-hum	Seesaw	Wig-wag
Flimflam	Knickknack	Shilly-shally	Zig-zag

____

____

____

____

____

Complete the following poem-starter:

Billy Beachum loved to play baseball.
He bought a bat; he bought a ball.

____

____

____

 © Educational Impressions, Inc.

Alliteration

Choose a consonant. Use a dictionary to make a list of twenty words beginning with that consonant.

LETTER: _______

Use as many of the words from your list as you can in a poem.

© Educational Impressions, Inc.

Assonance and Consonance

Assonance is the repetition of the same or similar vowel sounds with dissimilar consonant sounds. In other words, the vowels rhyme. Poets use assonance to create musical effects in poetry. To the reader or listener of a poem with assonance, the poem just sounds right. *That* and *hat* rhyme, but *that* and *task* are examples of assonance.

The following two lines are from "The Altercation," Activity No. 28A.

Line 4: "You don't say?"
Line 5: The sheriff's deputy reset his hat,

In Line 4 "you" and "don't" are examples of assonance.
In Line 5 "sheriff's," "deputy," and "reset" are examples of assonance.

Reread "The Altercation." Find at least three other examples of assonance in the poem.

____

____

Consonance is the repetition of consonant sounds, especially at the ends of stressed syllables with dissimilar vowel sounds; pet-sat-not and neck-kick-back, for example. (Another meaning of "consonance" is "an agreeable combination of musical tones.")

Find two or more examples of consonance in "The Altercation."

____

Write a short poem using assonance and consonance.

____

____

____

____

____

____

What are the examples of assonance in your poem?

____

What are the examples of consonance in your poem?

____

 © Educational Impressions, Inc.

Part Five:

Getting and Developing Ideas

Teacher Directions

ACTIVITY NO. 29: GETTING AND DEVELOPING IDEAS

It is not necessary that students have ideas for topics before they start to write poems. What is necessary is that they start to put words on paper. Warm-up activities, if used for warm-up and not as a substitute for the lesson itself, can help students get started.

OH UP; OH DOWN

My students respond well to a physical warm-up that we call "Oh up; oh down." Have students stand with fingers interlaced, palms outward, and arms straight in front. When you say, "Oh up," have them extend their arms above their heads and stretch their bodies. When you say, "Oh down," have them bring their arms (with their fingers still interlaced) back down to the front. Then have them bend their bodies at the waist so that they are parallel to the floor and stretch their arms as far to the front as possible. Next have them unlink their fingers and stretch their arms, keeping their bodies bent at the waist. Students then interlace their fingers behind their backs and, with their heads lowered toward the floor, stretch as high as possible. "Oh up; oh down" can be repeated three to five times, but no more. On the last "oh down" have students hold their last position until they think of an idea. As soon as they think of an idea, they sit down and start to write. If a student doesn't get an idea within a minute, hand him or her a slip of paper with three choices on it. Chances are the student will quickly come up with his or her own idea.

KENNINGS

A **kenning** is a metaphorical compound word or phrase used in Old English and Old Norse poetry. Examples are *swan road* for ocean; *home of the whale* for the sea; a *house guardian* for a dog; and a *hand house* for a glove. Have the students get into small groups and write kennings as a warm-up activity. Keep a list of words on hand to use for this activity. Spend no more than five minutes, if that long.

WORD PICTURES

The meanings of some words or suggestions of particular characteristics of the things named can be shown in the way the words are written. Short poems can be made from these words, or the activity can be used strictly for warm-up.

MaMa giraffe
stretched her Neck
to reach the Next
Limb for a tasty Morsel
to feed her family.

© Educational Impressions, Inc.

MIND-MAPPING (WEBBING, BRAIN-MAPPING, CLUSTERING), OUTLINING AND LISTING

Ideas can be developed in at least three different ways. Encourage your students to use the method best suited to them. Put the following example of mind-mapping on the board for your students. Have the class offer suggestions for the blank spaces.

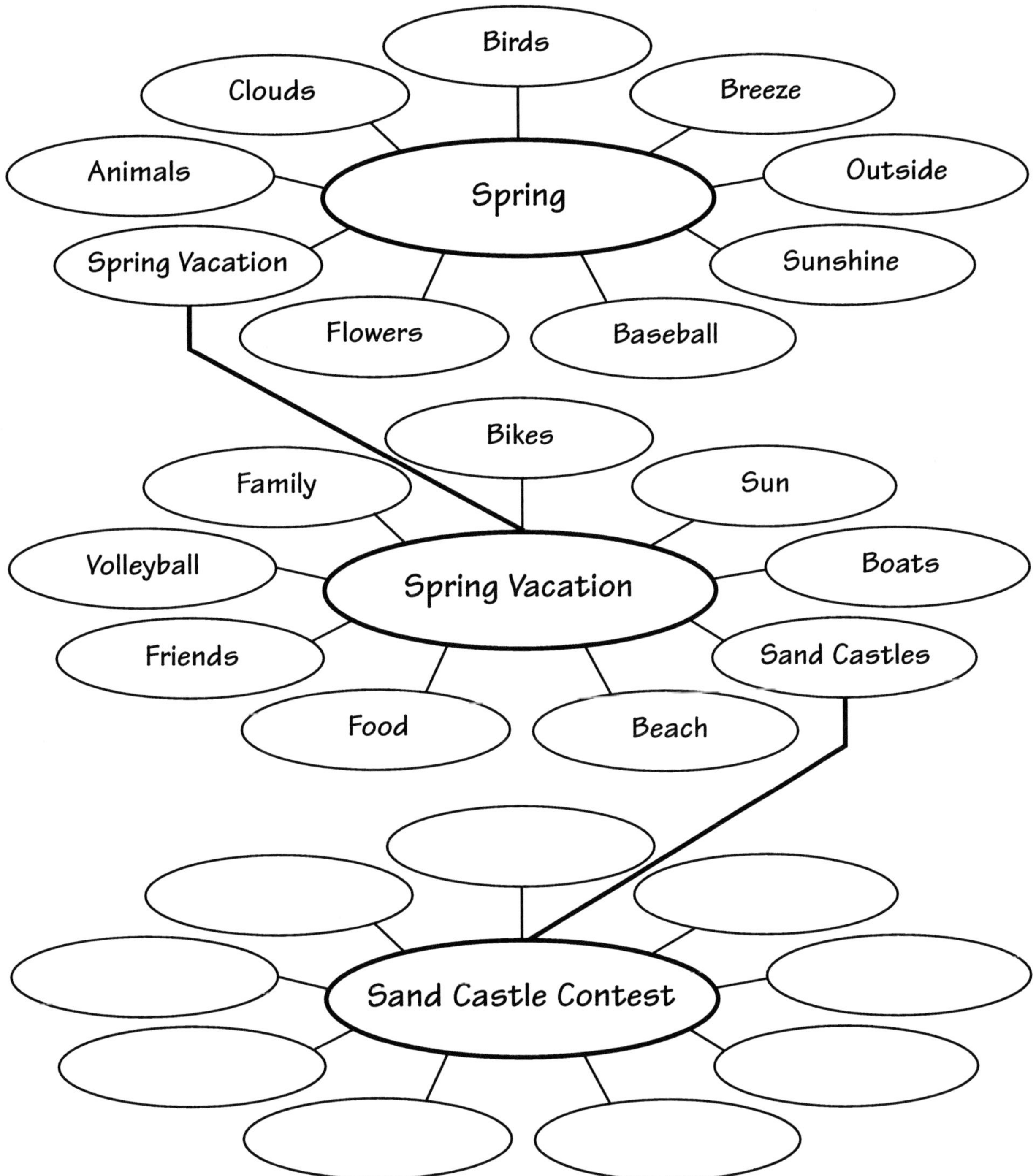

REWRITING

Rewriting (polishing, tweaking) is necessary for a finished poem. Encourage students to ask themselves the following questions: In what ways might I make this a better poem? Is there a better way to say this? Does the sound echo the sense? Have I said what I want to say in the way I want to say it?

Getting and Developing Ideas

Ideas for writing poetry come from a variety of sources. Sometimes ideas will simply pop into your head and you won't know their origins. At other times, ideas will develop from your daily contacts with people and things. Then there are those times when the idea box is empty. When that happens, if you have kept a literary journal (diary), you can use it for stored ideas.

I. GETTING IDEAS: The following are suggestions to help get the ideas flowing.

1. Brainstorm with a partner topics for a poem.
2. Flip through magazines and newspapers for topics of interest.
3. Free write. Jot down whatever comes into your mind.
4. The seasons and holidays are always good topics for poems.
5. Nature has been a topic of poetry since the beginning of poetry.
6. Birth, growing, aging, dying, and all in between are suitable topics.
7. Love in all its many forms is never out of style. Do try to avoid the "he/she loved me and left me and now I'm crying" genre of poetry.
8. Friendships and all relationships are good for ideas.
9. Observe people, animals, and situations for ideas.
10. Think about what you like to do. What are your interests and hobbies? What sports do you play? Of what organizations are you a member?
11. Think about your personality type. Are you a day person or a night person? Do you keep your room neat or messy? Are you afraid of snakes? Do you have any other phobias?
12. List your likes and dislikes.
13. Mind-mapping (webbing, brain-mapping, clustering) can help.
14. Make a list or an outline.

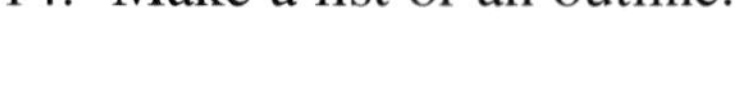

 © Educational Impressions, Inc.

II. FOCUSING: Zero in on one topic. It can be the one that appeals to you the most and/or the one that you already know the most about and that you think you can develop.

III. ADDING DETAILS: After you have chosen your topic, start adding details. You may use the techniques of mind-mapping, outlining, or list-making. Use vivid, specific words. Add specific words to the following list:

GENERAL	**SPECIFIC**
Cold day	Frigid, crisp day
Good	Perfect for…
Having a good time	______________________________
Fun	______________________________
Great!	______________________________

EXAMPLE OF LISTING:

RED BARN
Spring morning
Rusted tin roof
Red-tailed hawk riding on thermals above
Rambling red rose climbing one side almost obscuring the window
Green (brand) tractor under shed
Tabby cat at door watching the border collie
Dew
Wind chimes hanging from a corner of the barn

Finish the following list:

SCHOOL PLAYGROUND
Morning break
May (or other month or season)
Girls jumping rope
Boys ______________________________________

____

____

____

____

IV. SOUND AND SENSE: As you write your poem, remember that the sound should echo the meaning. One way to check the meaning of your poem is to **paraphrase** it in prose form. A paraphrase is a restatement of the text designed to make the meaning as clear as possible. The best way to check the sound of your poem is to **read it aloud** to yourself or to someone else. You may also want to have someone else read your poem to you. After you have checked your poem for both sound and sense, you will probably need to do some rewriting.

A HODGE-PODGE OF POSSIBLE TOPICS

These topics are in no particular order.

Time capsule: What is put in the capsule? Why? Who is expected to find it? What are the expected reactions?
Messages: from my cat or dog; from my great-great-grandfather; from George Washington; from a bottle; etc.
How to cook ______________________
In my backyard…
Remembering…
Popcorn: popping it; smelling it; eating it
Packing it all away: end of season; moving; outgrowing; growing up; going to college
Special anniversary…
Present and past…
Anticipation…
Mosquitoes
Pencils, crayons, or pens
Friends, old and new
Night sounds
Smells
Libraries
Books
Mythology
Seasons and special times of the year
Waking up or going to bed
After school, weekends, or school vacations
Origin of last name
Meaning of first name
Weather: rain, snow, heat, cold, thunderstorms, etc.
Famous last words as poem starters:
    Jump right in; the water's great.
    This won't hurt a bit.
    I'll only be gone a little while.
    Etc.
Bored people are boring
Meaning of a rainbow
Sunshine after a week of rain
Writing valentines or greeting-card messages
Writing Burma Shave Poetry (Look it up.)
Complete the following:
    I sneezed a sneeze,
    Then I coughed.
ADD OTHERS

 © Educational Impressions, Inc.

Part Six:

Poetry Showcase

© Educational Impressions, Inc.

POETRY SHOWCASE

Teacher Directions

In addition to having students read their poetry aloud in class, there are numerous ways that students' poetry can be showcased.

POETRY NOTEBOOK

Have students keep a poetry notebook that is divided into three sections. In one section they will keep copies of their original poetry. In the second they will keep copies of poems they like which were written by other poets, including their classmates. The third section will be used for notes.

POETRY MAGAZINE

With computer word-processing programs and copying machines it is easy to produce a classroom poetry magazine. Regular letter-size paper can be used and stapled three times on the left side. Legal-size or letter-size paper can be folded in the middle and stapled with a saddle stapler. Heavier weight paper can be used as covers.

POETS' CORNER

A corner of the classroom can be turned into a poets' corner. The walls can be covered with poems by students. Booklets or magazines of students' work can be made available.

THE (YOUR SCHOOL NAME) CAFÉ

With the aid of other teachers, administrators, parents, and students set up a (Your School Name) Café for poetry reading. A corner of the library, a corner of the cafeteria, a dead-end hall, an empty classroom (wouldn't that be nice?), or some other place in your school could be set up as a place where students come to read their poetry aloud to others.

POETRY SLAMS

Poetry slamming is a fairly new literary movement that began in Chicago; spread to San Francisco, New York, and Boston; and then spread throughout the rest of the states. It is a competition in which poets read their works aloud to an audience. Poets **slam** the other competitors with poetry and with words, but the main idea of a Poetry Slam is to get original poetry read aloud. There is a slam master who conducts the poetry slamming and three or more judges who choose first-, second-, and third-place winners and as many honorable mentions as the slam master wants. Make your own rules, or better yet, let your students make the rules. Poetry Slams can be conducted in your classroom and/or with other language arts/English classes. Just make sure that all rules are understood before you start. If you want more information about Poetry Slams, look the subject up on the World Wide Web. (Note: In this sense *slam* means to use poetry as a weapon—to "hit" the competition with the power of words.)

POETRY READINGS

After students have enough poems ready, you might like to arrange for them to read their poems to other classes, to the PTA, at faculty meetings, at district teachers' meetings, at nursing homes, and/or to civic groups.

© Educational Impressions, Inc.

RADIO AND TELEVISION

A local radio station will probably give your students air time for some poetry reading. The local access cable station will probably do the same.

INTERCOM SYSTEM

Make arrangements for your students to read their poetry over the school intercom. If you have closed-circuit television in your school, arrange for your students to have a special spot to read their poetry.

CANDLELIGHT (OR FLASHLIGHT) POETRY READING

Have the poetry readers line up at the front of a darkened room with their backs turned to the audience. The readers should be wearing dark clothes if possible. Each reader has a candle or a flashlight. To begin, the person on one end lights his/her candle (or flips on the flashlight), turns to face the audience, and reads his/her original poem. The next person in line lights his/her candle or flashlight, turns, and reads his/her poem. This continues with the third, fourth, fifth, etc., until all poems have been read. All the candles and flashlights remain lit until the last poem has been read. At that time, all the candles are blown out or flashlights turned off at the same time. Music adds a nice touch, but it is best done "live."

TAPING POETRY

You can arrange to have students record their poems on tape recorders or video cameras to play in class.

POETRY WRITE-A-THON

Discuss the terms "marathon" and "telethon" (Jerry Lewis's Labor Day Telethon, for example) with your students. In my area we also have walk-a-thons, rock-a-thons, skip-a-thons, and other "a-thons" to raise money for charitable organizations. You might like to use the poetry write-a-thon to raise funds for a special project.

Decide on a length of time, but keep it under two weeks. Encourage students to come up with their own topics, but provide some suggestions. Also give out the following rules.

CONTEST RULES:

1. Poems must be legibly written in blue or black ink, typed, or printed.

2. Poems must be written on only one side of regular letter-size paper.

3. Names must be included. They may be at the top, right side of the paper, below the title, or at the end. You decide.

4. Students may submit ____ (you determine the number) poems. All students must submit at least one poem.

Poems may be bound into a booklet, displayed on a bulletin board, or presented in any other way.

BULLETIN BOARDS AND OTHER PUBLIC DISPLAYS

Hallway walls, lunchroom walls, libraries, and other areas in the school can serve as areas for displaying students' poems. The public library, local banks, grocery stores, city halls, county courthouses, district school offices, and other public buildings will sometimes welcome a display of students' poetry, especially if a parent works there or if parents do business there.

Bulletin boards are always good places to display poetry. The following are possible headlines:

- Spotlight on Poetry
- Poetry Festival
- Try It; You'll Like It (Poetry for the Masses)
- Swinging with Poetry
- Poetry Highlights
- Poetry Slam
- Poetry Galore
- I Can't Believe It's Poetry!
- Word Pictures

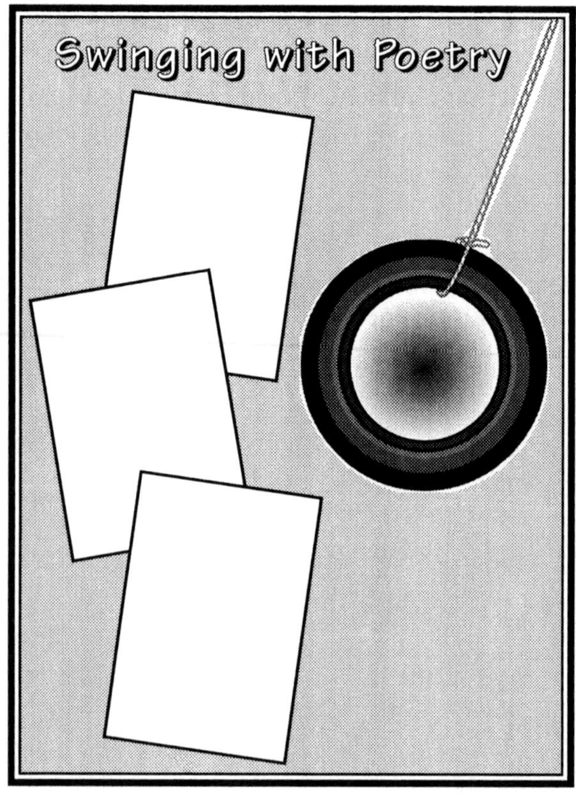

 © Educational Impressions, Inc.

Part Seven:

Student Poetry

SUMMER

Silently coming after spring,
Unbowed by winter.
Memories of
Morning glories, mimosas, and magnolias
Elbowing thoughts of school away,
Replacing them with thoughts of play.

Jeff Atkinson, Grade 7
Demetrius Thomaston, Grade 8

AUTUMN

All the leaves floating down,
Under the trees and
To the ground.
Unmasking
More and more trees, leaving
Nature in naked splendor.

Roger Harrod, Grade 5
Betty Parmer, Grade 8

FLAG

Flying, floating in the sky,
Like a bird hovering high,
All the day and all the night.
Gracious, it's a beautiful sight.

Jeff Atkinson, Grade 7
Demetrius Thomaston, Grade 8

MUSHROOM

Made by God,
Under the trees,
Shady and damp,
Hiding from me,
Rapidly appearing,
Overnight I see,
Once a spore, now,
Magnificent to be.

David Crowe, Grade 5
Christy Jackson, Grade 4
Loretta Loftin, Grade 8

RIFLE

Remorse bringer,
Irreversible action,
Fired indiscriminately,
Launching eternity,
Everlasting death.

Ralph Caldwell, Grade 6
Keith Runels, Grade 7

ADOLESCENT

Always active,
Dancing, dating, daring,
Obstinate,
Loveable and ludicrous,
Eager, edgy,
Sensitive, self-conscious,
Careless, challenging, cunning,
Energetic, exciting, exasperating,
Naughty nuisances,
Tantalizing teenagers!

Polly Crowder, Grade 8
Betty Goodson, Grade 8
Angela Lovelace, Grade 5
Candi Marshall, Grade 5

I WISH I WERE A MOUNTAIN

I wish I were a mountain,
So I'd stand so tall and proud,
So my snow-white cap and majestic peak
Would always draw a crowd.

I wish I were a mountain,
So I'd stand so big and high.
When people stop and look at me,
They would always have to sigh.

I wish I were a mountain,
So everyone could see
How beautiful a mountain is,
But for now I think I'll just be me.

Scott Smith, Grade 8

© Educational Impressions, Inc.

IF I COULD...

If I could grab a piece of time,
  I'd put it in a sack
And keep it hidden in my drawer,
  Way far in the back.
If I could catch a ray of sun,
  I'd wrap it up real tight
And keep it stuffed under my bed
  To keep me warm at night.
If I could cut out a patch of sky,
  I'd seal it in a jar,
And every night before my prayers,
  I'd add a little star.
If I could bag a tiny breeze,
  I'd hang it over here,
And now and then I'd let it out,
  To whisper in my ear.

Kim Crawford, Grade 9

FUTURE PLANS

If I could sail,
If I could go,
If I could be my own.

If I were old,
If I were wise,
  I wish I were all of me,
  Belonging to none,
  Completely free.

Be it truth,
Or be it dreams,
If only I could...
I wish I could be...

Megan Davis, Grade 10

THE SKY

It is best that
The sky does not have a ceiling.
We haven't a broom
Long enough
To knock down
The cobwebs.

Roger Warren, Grade 9

THE PARADE

Life is a parade,
People marching to the music,
Everyone wanting to be the best,
Searching for the fame and fortune
That life holds hidden.
Each knowing his position
And his routine,
Practicing for perfection.
Yet it is those few
Who are out of step
That make the parade fascinating.

Renee Ayers, Grade 9

SEASONS

All I like is—
  Summer,
    Spring,
      Fall,
And that is all.

Pam Hoag, Grade 3

THE INVASION

The wind playfully teases the leaves and
  flowers.
Mockingbirds, robins, and meadowlarks
  join their voices in symphonic poems.
Honeysuckle, sweet shrubs, and wild roses
  aromatize the air.
    Footsteps!
The mockingbirds, sweet shrubs, and wild
  roses withhold their perfume.
Man—The Invader.

Leigh Cook, Grade 9

MYSELF

Some people think I'm daring;
Others just say I'm all right.
I think I'm kind of neighborly,
'Cause I don't like to fuss and fight.

David Adamson, Grade 6

© Educational Impressions, Inc.

THEM SMART KIDS

How about them smart kids,
Ain't they cool,
Making straight A's
All the way through school?

Studying at night
And all during the day,
They keep studying
While others play.

Look at them smart kids,
Out of school,
Got a good job,
Ain't nobody's fool.

Them hard-working smart kids
Ain't so dumb.
They don't sit on their butts
And twiddle their thumbs.

How to be a smart kid,
There ain't nothing to it.
Just grab you a book
And sock your brain to it.

David Hosey, Grade 9

WIND

I am wind; I cover all.
I fill cracks and crannies, bottles, and jars;
I am sucked through Cuban cigars;
I whistle through trees and across buildings tall;
I am wind; I cover all.

I am wind; I cover all.
I move kites and sails, balls and balloons;
I waft caterpillars bound in lacy cocoons;
I storm around corners and down chimneys tall;
I am wind; I cover all.

I am wind; I cover all.
I stir leaves and hair, flags and flowers;
I shift clouds around tops of towers;
I whine through valleys and across mountains tall;
I am wind; I cover all.

David Hosey, Grade 9

DAYDREAMING

Look behind the rainbow and there you'll find me.
I'm not doing my work; I'm daydreaming, you see!
I'm building castles, massive and tall.
They are so towering and I am so small.
In my dreams, I am the supreme ruler.
Even in summer things are cooler.
I have everything in my dreams.
I never work, just lick the cream.
I make myself different, not like now.
I do things my parents don't allow.
Take a trip on a rainbow slide.
Welcome to this castle where I abide!

Carol Jackson, Grade 9

MIRROR

The mirror is the magic of man.
For his quest throughout time
Has been to see himself,
To know himself as others do,
And the mirror is his tool.
However, he must remember
That the mirror shows everything
Exactly in reverse.

Debra Newell, Grade 9

THRILLS

I'd love to tame a wild horse,
Jump into the sea from rocky cliffs,
Soar high in a plane, then fall to earth,
Race at unbearable speeds.
I am not self-destructive.
It just fascinates me to see
What will make my heart beat faster.
Nothing scares me;
I'm never intelligent enough to see the danger.

Renee Ayers, Grade 9

© Educational Impressions, Inc.

IF THE WORLD WERE ENDING TOMORROW!

If the world were ending tomorrow,
I'd be very busy today!
(That is, of course, if I knew about the end!)

I'd be getting everything off my chest,
Then I'd apologize for blowing my top!
I'd be finishing all my business,
Like algebra and science homework,
Or I might finish my novel
And see about getting it published.
I'd be going places—
Six Flags, Disneyland, or Terry's house.

What's that?
You say the world IS ending tomorrow?
Then hurry and get out of here!
With you under my feet
It'd take more than a day
Just to decide what to WEAR!

Jeni Giles, Grade 9

AWAKENING

I emerged into consciousness,
Momentarily suspended between dream
and reality,
My brain filled with a collage
Of leftover dreams
And pieces of yesterday's realities.
Momentarily I hovered,
Existing in neither world,
With a tenuous grip on the poetic images
That swarmed, half remembered,
Throughout my brain.
My grip relaxed,
Leaving the bright rays of the early morning
sun
To wipe away all traces of the images
That lingered within my mind.

Linda Bowman, Grade 10

THE BRANCH JUST BEYOND MY HOUSE

Bending and twisting by poplars and elms
Is the branch just beyond my house.
Water churns on the rocks—
Splashing and sparkling endlessly.
A fallen leaf slides with the currents,
Like an ancient galleon of the past,
Sailing on cool ripples.

Peaceful sounds reign—
Trickling,
Peaceful sounds—
Lilting,
Envied by the earth and all inhabitants.

Smiling green eyes cast upon the water,
Reflect—
All the good times.
The smiles shared.
The light and fire that once
Lived
In someone's heart.
But still—
The branch just beyond my house
Moves one.

Roger Warren, Grade 10

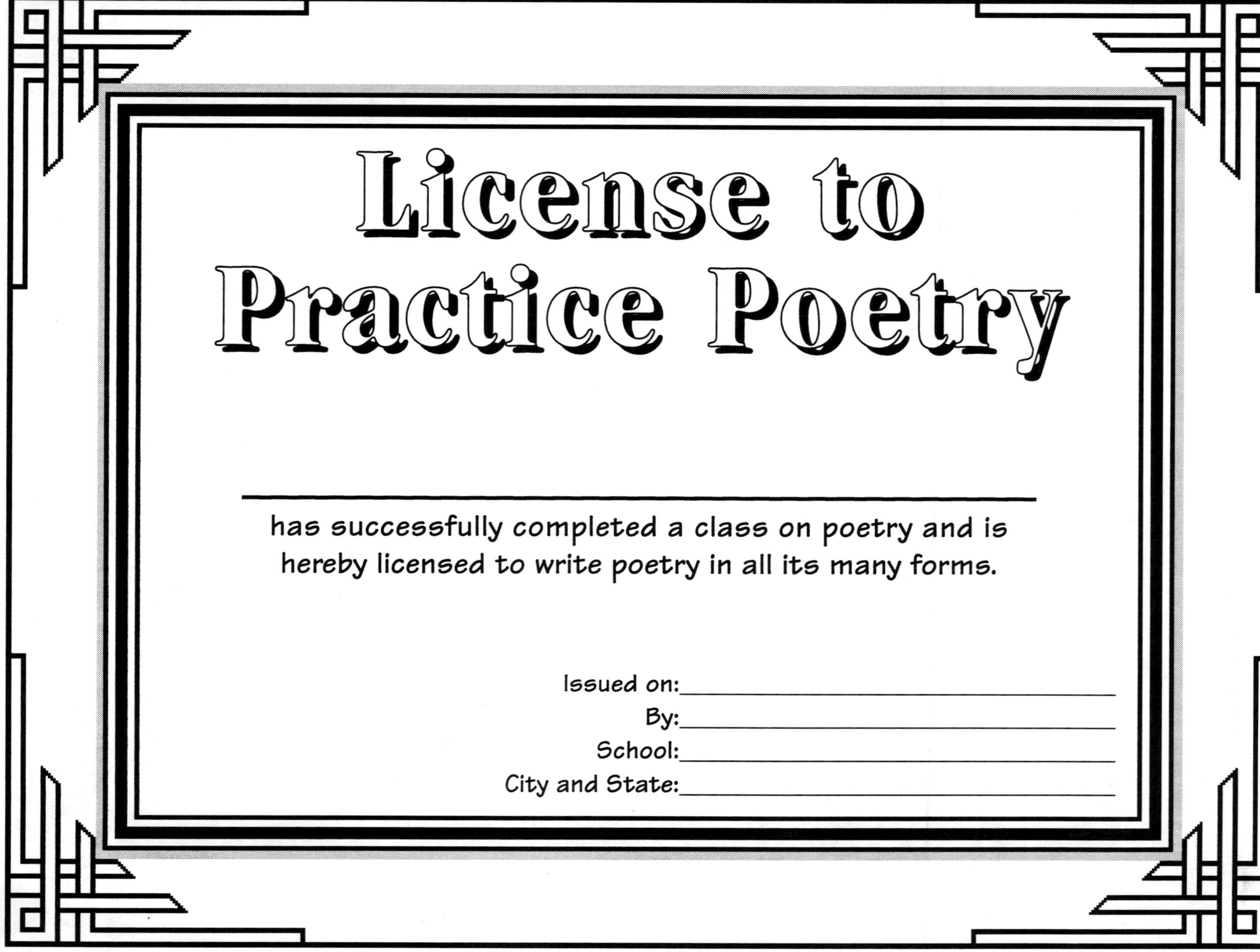

License to Practice Poetry

____

has successfully completed a class on poetry and is hereby licensed to write poetry in all its many forms.

Issued on: ____________________

By: ____________________

School: ____________________

City and State: ____________________

© Educational Impressions, Inc.